The Politics of Worship

The Politics of
WORSHIP

Reforming the Language
and Symbols of Liturgy

WILLIAM JOHNSON EVERETT

UNITED CHURCH PRESS
Cleveland, Ohio

United Church Press, Cleveland, Ohio 44115
© 1999 by William Johnson Everett

Printed in the United States of America on acid-free paper

04 03 02 01 00 99   5 4 3 2 1

Library of Congress Cataloging-in-Publication Data

Everett, William Johnson.
   The politics of worship : reforming the language and symbols of liturgy /
William Johnson Everett.
      p. cm.
   Includes bibliographical references.
   ISBN 0-8298-1341-1 (pbk. : alk. paper)
   1. Liturgical language. I. Title.
BV178.E94 1999
264'.001'4—dc21
                                                99-34493
                                                CIP

Contents

Preface

IN THE MID-1980s I wrote a book about how we might move from kingship symbolism to the symbolism of democracy, republics, and federalism as the framework for thinking about Christian ethics.[1] As soon as I finished the book I began to realize more profoundly how the language of feudal monarchy still pervades our worship. Not only do Bible readings and hymns powerfully convey these symbols, but the way many of us kneel for receiving communion or for praying, as well as the way the church year is arranged to celebrate the birth, death, and resurrection of a king, depends deeply on a commitment to a feudal monarchical political order.

This quickly became more than a personal intellectual quandary. Ordinary monarchical worship became as painful for me as traditional worship is for anyone with feminist ears. This intense discomfort drove my wife, Sylvia, who is an artist of religious and spiritual themes, and me to lead a variety of small worship groups in order to live into the symbolism of contemporary politics as the voice of our prayers, songs, gestures, and movements. Our efforts were first nurtured by our experiences in Roman Catholic parishes during my time teaching in Milwaukee at St. Francis Seminary. Roman liturgical tradition—for all its patriarchy—bore with it not only a sense of drama and order but a sensibility for symbolism that was like water in the dry desert of my Protestant world of words. Subsequent projects in Atlanta and then at Andover Newton Theological School in Newton Centre, Massachusetts, further advanced our search for worship that was both aesthetically powerful and ethically congruent. Out of these experiences came the raw ingredients for this little book.

These brief chapters seek to do two things. First, I lay out the rationale for such a quest. Why is it important to try to change the political metaphors and symbols of our worship? What would such a shift entail? On what basis would we do it? What principles should guide us? The first six chapters form the theoretical foundation for reconstructing our worship. People who like to move logically and intellectually through a problem should simply begin here with chapter 1. Those who prefer to begin with practical experience should turn first to chapter 7.

In that chapter, I move more directly to the practical aspects of change. Drawing on elements of our worship experiments and experiences, I walk through an imagined worship activity informed by contemporary political symbolism. This fantasy provides practical examples of how we might proceed in practice. For an additional taste of a practical entry, readers might choose to begin with the appendix titled "A Conversation with President Jesus." As these theoretical and practical proposals inevitably raise a number of difficult questions, I conclude, in chapter 8, with some of the critical questions people have raised in light of these experiences and perspectives.

While this book is written as a Christian argument, it also seeks to engage Jews and others who share the broad biblical tradition, for we confront similar issues. For all of us, this essay only begins a conversation, indeed, for many people a rather emotional argument! If the present course of worship, even with efforts at gender inclusivity, is painful for me, so are the changes I propose for others.

I hope this short book can help people begin the process of thinking about this challenge and eventually reshaping their worship life so it can speak the language of longing for more adequate republics knit together by strong covenants with the peoples and other creatures of this fragile world.

Acknowledgments

WORSHIP IS A COLLECTIVE endeavor, as is any effort to reflect on it and make changes in it. I am grateful to many people for participating in this search with me. Above all I am deeply grateful to my wife, Sylvia, who has done so much to introduce me to the aesthetic dimensions of symbols and rituals as well as to help me clarify and express my thoughts for a wider audience. Her artistic contributions to our experiments in worship have accompanied every step of this journey.

For taking time through letters and conversation about earlier drafts of this book I am indebted especially to Douglas Bax, Paul Clayton, James Crawford, Paul Deats, Gerd Decke, John DeGruchy, Margaret Donaldson, Daniel Elazar, Gordon Freeman, Vigen Guroian, Sheldon Harr, Heidi King, Mary Luti, Susan Murtha-Smith, Jyoti Sahi, Nancy and Kenneth Sehested, Bennett and Mary Page Sims, and Kenneth Smits. My thanks also go to Howard Hanger and the Jubilee! Community of Asheville, North Carolina, for encouragement and inspiration along the way. I am also grateful to people who collaborated with me in worship at Briarcliff United Methodist Church in Atlanta; at the United Parish of Auburndale, Massachusetts; at Sweet Fellowship Baptist Church, Clyde, North Carolina; and at the Rondebosch United Church in Cape Town, South Africa. In addition, numerous colleagues, students, and staff at Andover Newton Theological School have prodded, encouraged, and vigorously criticized both my practices and thoughts through experiences of worship, debate, and conversation.

The circle of contributors to this work is broad, and this list only encompasses a few who have left their fingerprints on it. I hope this publication will extend the conversation further—another earnest of the great republic to which God calls us.

CHAPTER ONE

Beyond the Worship
of "Kingafap"

OVER THE PAST TWENTY YEARS the language of Christian worship has increasingly reflected the desire to include women and groups marginalized by the forms of worship rooted in the Bible and in European traditions. New hymnals have struggled to change male-dominated language and to eliminate prejudicial metaphors so the voices and faces of women as well as men from all races and cultures can find expression. People have struggled to use new metaphors for God to expand our imaginations, introducing themes not only from women's experience but from nature. Such a major overhaul continues to percolate through attempts to renovate worship in many religious traditions.

The Methodist composer Brian Wren writes with wit and insight about the ponderous inheritance of hymns filled with the language of "Kingafap"—King-God-Almighty-Father-Protector.[1] This metaphorical construct pervades our hymns and prayers, narrowing our vision of God to an idolatrous celebration of male dominance. As Wren eloquently and insightfully argues, this narrow set of metaphors for the holy and mysterious Creator both distorts our understanding of the Holy One and reinforces structures of power and authority that exclude women and the creatures who are partners in our life.

Wren's critique has led him to generate hymns that use many names for God to expand our imagination, opening us up to surprising new revelations of God and undermining the exclusive claims of patriarchy. This effort to include all sorts and conditions of people in the way we pray, sing, and ritualize can be seen as part of the surge toward democratization that has been under way around the world for some two centuries. Inclusivity as a norm for worship language and ritual thus brings democratic values into worship. However, the main thrust of reform, as with Wren's work, focuses on issues of gender, ecology, and race, not on political form. Patriarchal monarchy is rejected not because it is monarchy—a form of governance—but because it is sexist. Nature is included not because it constitutes itself as land—the territory of a common life—but as a motherlike generativity.

Wren himself tweaks our interest in the questions of political order when he speaks of a "republican King," one who does not simply vacate his throne for an excursion to rescue humanity, only to return to the throne in splendor after a spellbinding resurrection. Wren's King-God finally sets aside his throne altogether to become not a president but a gardener. The nurturing claims of nature—both for humanity and for the whole creation—are the lodestones of his theological compass.

Thus, to say Wren's efforts to reform our worship language and symbols are democratic is somewhat of an interpretation. To see the move away from exclusively male imagery as political, however, should not be surprising. Indeed, the modern development of republican political theories, which begins with John Locke's *Two Treatises on Government* (1690), rests on an extended and rigorous rejection of biblically grounded patriarchy. Locke rejects patriarchal appeals to the Bible not because of their sexism, though he throws in a few barbs on that score, but because they arrogate to one person in the paternal role the civil governance that should be shared by all adults. They maintain people as children before a representative father, who administers the commonwealth like his own household. To get at the political question of public governance, Locke has to attack the symbolism of patriarchy. From this point, a democratic ethos begins to develop that gradually extends its power not only into realms of governance but into the home. Modern feminism, then, can be understood as a further development of what began as a political claim, now extended into the domestic, economic, and ecological spheres. In the process, the struggle against patriarchy forgot its political roots and became a struggle over differentiation of the genders in the private sphere of intimacy, parenthood, and work. The major burden of my argument here is to recover this political heritage as the central language of theology and worship.

In this recovery the question of gender becomes a question of governance, and the question of inclusivity is reunited with the question of political authority. The efforts toward gender inclusivity have been crucial in inculcating the values of equality in the way we are being brought up, but this step has its distinct limits. The limits of the strategy of inclusivity become visible in the translations of the language of lordship, kingship, and kingdom in hymns and prayers. In an effort to be gender inclusive, "lord" becomes "sovereign," "kingdom" becomes "realm," and "kingship" becomes "reign." The king moves over to accommodate a queen, of whatever race, but the structure of monarchy that accompanied patriarchy remains intact. The occupants of the castle have become more diverse, even "representative," but the castle remains to dominate our political horizon.

Take, for instance, the classic hymn "All Hail the Power of Jesus' Name," now refurbished in the *New Century Hymnal*, probably the most thorough effort at inclusivity in recent years. The original Kingafap version reads:

> All hail the power of Jesus' name, let angels prostrate fall,
> Bring forth the royal diadem and crown Him Lord of all.
> Bring forth the royal diadem and crown Him Lord of all.

The inclusive version reads:

> All hail the power of Jesus' name, let angels prostrate fall;
> Bring forth the royal diadem, and crown Christ servant of all.
> Attend the Savior's sovereign claim, and crown Christ servant of all.[2]

Notice what has happened: In order to combat sexist language, references to "him" and "Lord" have been replaced, but the language of crowning, diadems, angelic prostration, thrones, and royalty survive the cut. The one effort to soften the royal imagery, in the third line of the inclusive version, turns to the language of sovereignty. While this begins to depart from the language of Kingafap, it remains within the conceptions of personal sovereignty typical of monarchical governance.

In a similar vein, take the hymn by Timothy Dwight, "I Love Thy Kingdom, Lord" (1801). The original first verse reads:

I love thy kingdom, Lord, the house of thine abode,
The church our blest Redeemer saved with his own precious blood.

The gender-inclusive version now reads:

We love your realm, O God, all places where you reign,
We recognize, with hope and joy, the world as your domain.[3]

Here the symbolic framework of feudal monarchy not only survives the inclusivity filter but is actually introduced where it had not even appeared in the original! The language of bloody redemption, which resonates both with classic sacrificial themes as well as with contemporary martyrdoms for true liberation, has been erased to lift up a theme of social transformation unconnected to the forms of political justice people know and seek to enhance in the real world of democracies, republics, and federations.

FROM GENDER TO GOVERNANCE

In the reformation of sexist language, worship leaders have extended the democratic impulse informing conceptions of gender justice but have themselves remained within the structures of monarchical political thought. Such an effort at gender inclusivity fails to grasp the political struggle within which antipatriarchal thought and values emerged. Efforts at inclusivity have generally been married to the domestic world of intimacy but divorced from the public world of governance. Thus, Christian worship remains an anomalous and nostalgic relic of feudal monarchy and empire—though inclusive of all aspiring sovereigns and subjects—within an increasing expanse of hopeful and struggling democracies, republics, and federations. However, it is in the struggle for genuine republics, stable federations, and constitutions rooted in doctrines of human rights that people are pouring out their lifeblood. It is in this struggle that the testimonies of faith are being cried and sung, yet our worship language still lies in feudal frames. We have replaced some words, but we have not changed the grammar or syntax.

As Brian Wren has pointed out, we need to move beyond the insertion of words to the composition of entirely new songs.[4] However, without a sense of what is at stake between competing political visions, we tend to remove all metaphors of political governance in order to deal with issues of gender and inclusivity. Because so much human anguish has arisen from the acts and policies of governments, we try to flee from all questions of governance into a domestic haven of personal relations or a garden of natural harmony. Rather than continue the struggle for more just forms of governance, we begin to assume that all politics is monarchical and equally coercive or hierarchical.

However, even in biblical times kingship was not the only possible form of governance. Indeed, the first book of Samuel sets forth the tension between governance by tribal councils within a confederation and governance by a king. This tension—between council and king, between polis and empire, between parliament and crown—courses throughout church history. It is this conflict that erupted once again in the Puritan revolutions that led to John Locke's republicanism, John Stuart Mill's liberalism, and the democratic socialism of Walter Rauschenbusch.

The struggle for democratic republics and against parental forms of government also molds much of the struggle against slavery, against the exclusion of women from public life, and for worker participation in the operation of business enterprises. In short, the biblical, historical, and contemporary furnaces of faith have been political. Biblical faith has always been a struggle over alternative forms of governance, whether in Genesis, Exodus, Jeremiah, Luke, or Revelation. Christian worship, I will argue here, must be seen in this political perspective if it is to sustain not only its religious tradition but also the visions of justice by which people are struggling to live today.

Without this step of recognizing the struggle over proper political order, this democratization of worship language cannot effectively engage people's wider aspirations, values, and commitments. This recognition moves us to symbolize in our worship life and language the structures of governance within which democratic inclusivity can actually function. The question we face is not merely about who should participate, but within what structures of authority and power they should reconcile their differences and work for common ends, especially for the care of the earth they share with each other and with future generations. With regard to the worship forms shaping and expressing this search for political justice, it is time to move from kingdom to republic as the metaphor of the new order of authority and power for which we long in faith.

This enterprise is only partially rational. Nothing is more deeply emotional and "pre-rational" than the symbols, rituals, forms, and phrases that shape our relation with the ultimate sources of meaning. The reasonable discourse of a book can only help us bring to consciousness some ways we might challenge, guide, and change the fundamental habits of our conversation with God. Moreover, changes in symbols, worship, and ritual emerge organically rather than mechanically. They can only flower under the right confluence of experience, need, hope, and commitment. Most of the seeds this book hopes to disseminate will not find such happy circumstance. But perhaps a few will scatter to a corner where other stewards might take up the task of nurture and advancement.

Such a political approach to worship involves seeing it from the standpoint of ethics. Ethical concerns have always accompanied the reform of worship under way in both Catholic and Protestant circles for the past sixty years. In the first chapter we will review that development as a quest for ethical integrity in worship. What I am proposing is that worship reform take on a new partner in its search for ethical integrity, namely political theory. Most discussion of worship has used either anthropology, mythology, or psychology as its partner. But to engage fruitfully both biblical tradition and the classic functions of worship, we need to address questions only political theory can raise. Lamentably, concern for political theory, as distinguished from the popular political cause of the moment, has not been central or even present in theological conversations about worship, even though the Bible and church history are permeated with such questions. By politics I do not mean merely the mobilization of people to achieve particular goals, but the whole scheme of governance we usually think of in terms of constitutional theory. That is, we need to think of worship in terms of its relation to our general ideas of how people ought to govern themselves. Grasping this close connection of worship to governance requires a certain perspective on worship itself. We have to think more clearly about the purposes of worship.

While worship usually serves many purposes, I will argue in chapter 3 that we ought to think of it primarily as the symbolic and dramatic rehearsal of the ultimate structure of just relationships that God—the author and source of justice—intends for all creatures of the cosmos. Worship is the fundamental way we articulate our sense of just and legitimate governance. This is why it has always contained both the power to absolutize an existing regime as well as to undermine it with the vision of a new and transcendent order.

Once we have taken on this political understanding of worship, we need to look critically at why and how Christians have remained monarchists in worship despite the republican and democratic revolutions of the past two centuries—especially among Christians who have enthusiastically supported these revolutions. If the biblical and theological arguments for democratic symbolism in worship are so strong, why have Christians persisted in the rehearsal of archaic forms of monarchy and patriarchy? In the examination of this question in chapter 4 we will see the profound ways in which worship has been individualized and psychologized, leading it far from its biblical roots or its historic meanings. Worship becomes therapy or archaic nostalgia rather than a rehearsal of the vibrant visions of an assembly longing for a new order of power and authority. It becomes so wedded to the private sphere of family and personal life that it forgets the challenges of public life still echoing in its own heritage.

In light of this change of perspective and this awareness of our history and present circumstances, we need to establish guidelines for regenerating our worship in order to reclaim its classic functions in a new voice. That is the task I address in chapters 5 and 6: How do we even talk about the key symbols and concepts of political life? How do we appropriate them critically? How can key commitments to republican and democratic life, to federal association among republics, and to religious hope for God's coming order of justice be woven into the tapestry of our worship life? How can we preserve the delicate tension between engaging the language of republics, democracies, federations, and constitutions while maintaining the critical judgment rooted in a transcendent, mysterious, and holy God? How can worship mediate the connection as well as the gulf between our anticipation of God's governance and God's ultimate aim? How can we speak the language of our deepest political convictions without simply singing the song of our own self-advancement?

Such a difficult task is an art, not a technique. It dwells in the particulars of acts, words, images, and songs. What are the practices that actually can cradle such a fresh vision of worship? The worship fantasy in chapter 7 takes us to the practical expression of this conception of worship reform. Once we reach the point of making specific decisions about how to refurbish the political symbols of worship, we then realize that every such effort is culturally specific and limited. The final chapter investigates questions of cultural context that deeply shape every effort at a worship that engages both our emotional roots and our ethical aspirations.

CHAPTER TWO

The Need for Integrity in Worship

THE SEARCH FOR INTEGRITY in worship has many dimensions and takes many forms. While aesthetic, theological, psychological, and cultural motives all figure strongly in the development of worship forms, ethical concerns have often been present in struggles for the reform of worship. Sometimes these ethical factors are left implicit or undeveloped, but when they are clearly introduced we have to ask not only what values and norms are being advanced but how ethical concerns should be related to aesthetics, psychology, theology, or culture. In order to get at these questions, we need to step back briefly to look at the development of worship reforms in the twentieth century.

WORSHIP REFORMS IN THE TWENTIETH CENTURY

Twentieth-century worship reform in liturgical churches began with the efforts of Benedictine groups in France and Germany to reclaim forms of chant, psalmody, and prayer from the medieval and early church. In a profound sense, this was a "traditional" move. By showing that the Catholic Church's received forms were actually historical accretions, both the canons of traditionalism and the hopes of reform could be served. While such efforts had many motives and purposes, certainly one among them was to reestablish the distinctiveness of the church over and against a decaying and increasingly destructive European political order. The autumn feast of Christ the King, for instance, was introduced by Pope Pius XI in 1925 to counter secularism as well as the totalitarian claims of fascist movements that tried to subordinate the church to their purposes.[1]

The most progressive among these reformers, such as Yves Congar, sought to explicate worship as the action of the whole church rather than its individual priests. They tried to recover the original meaning of church—ecclesia—as an assembly. Such endeavors finally came to fruition in the Second Vatican Council (1961–64), whose pastoral constitutions led to worship reforms throughout the church. Altars were moved away from the wall to become communion tables. Priests faced the congregation in order to create a circle of the assembly around the table, and the laity became increasingly involved in the conduct of worship. These moves were a step toward a more democratic and participatory form of worship—one necessary for a church that would have to rest increasingly on the voluntary commitments of its members.

To reinforce this focus on the whole community, liturgical scholars began to draw on the work of anthropologists, who lifted up the way ritual life is inextricably tied to the life of whole communities, not just their mediated relation to God. The works of Evans-Pritchard, Emile Durkheim, Bronislaw Malinowski, and more recently Mary Douglas and Victor Turner have exerted an enormous impact on both Catholic and Protestant liturgical studies.[2] They see worship as a natural part of human life, as the means by which communities preserve their key values and orientations, pass them on to new members, and deal with the anxiety provoked by war, disease, life transitions, and death. Through their eyes, worship is the primary means for communities to integrate the different aspects of people's lives into a meaningful whole. It is the expression of a natural religious need in all societies.

With these arguments from "natural religion," liturgical scholars could press for worship forms aimed at broadscale participation and social relationships rather than focus on an individualistic and otherworldly cult administered by priests who are separated from the ordinary life of the community. Moreover, these anthropological studies, with their focus on "primitive" communities, did not deal at all with the role of the state in religion, since these communities have no "state." Thus, worship could be seen apart from the apparatus of state support so deeply embedded in European church life. At least in principle it could be unwound from its long and now deadly embrace in the arms of Christendom. Christian worship could be liberated from its function of celebrating European monarchy, empire, or aristocracy. The church's worship could then be developed out of its own independent life, something crucial to its future integrity and survival in Europe but a long-accustomed reality in America. In short, worship could be related more directly to the ongoing ethical life of the Christian community. The concept of "community" tended to ignore distinctions between the church and other institutions, not to mention the highly pluralistic associational life of urban industrial people, but these institutional concerns were less important than the simple, more general effort to relocate liturgy within people's social life.

This recovery of popular participation in worship was not without significance for people (the "demos") in both church and society, whether in Europe, Latin America, or North America. Changes in worship resonated with movements for liberation in South America as well as movements for church reform in the north. The North American Liturgical Conference, for instance, eventually foundered on its espousal of increasingly radical social reforms through worship.

Among Protestants, worship reform has first involved a movement from exclusive fixation on "the Word" in preaching and teaching to a cultivation of the symbolic life of all the senses, especially in the recovery of the Eucharist as central to Christian worship but also in the use of the visual arts, dance, and drama. While Catholics sought to recover the Word in biblical study and preaching, Protestants sought to recover the symbolic sense of the liturgy. While Catholics tried to revive the life of local communities, Protestants tried, through lectionaries and celebrations of the church year, to link independent congregations to the wider church. Just as history and anthropology have been crucial for Catholic reforms, so psychology and the arts have been for Protestants. The work of Don Saliers, for instance, has focused intensively on the way worship shapes the religious affections, indeed our entire motivational and emotional structure.[3] More recently, a number of Protestant seminaries have established programs in theology and the arts to enhance worship and spirituality.

Even in this shift, Protestantism generally remains committed to a focus on the regeneration of people and conversion of individuals in an experience of awakening and revival. These individuals are then called to bear fruit in actions of love and justice and mercy in their daily lives. Thus, the American Social Gospel movement of the late nineteenth and early twentieth centuries drew on the tradition of personal conversion but extended it to the transformation of the emerging corporate systems of late industrial society. Social action could draw on the motivational capital invested in worship experiences that sought to repeat and ritually represent the revivals at the heart of American evangelical traditions. Some of the renewed interest in worship from Protestants arises in the collapse of this connection between revival, worship, and social action. Worship can no longer energize converted people, who will in turn convert their world. Social action has spent the spiritual capital of revival. Reconnecting the two aspects of worship and social transformation requires a reconstitution both of worship life and of social action. For Protestants, worship reform requires a new conception of the connection of worship to spirituality and ethics.

In spite of their differences, we see many points of increasing convergence between Catholic and Protestant worship perspectives and practices. This is especially true in North America, with its ecumenical institutions for theological education and the high rate of intermarriage and movement among denominations in a religious world governed more by markets and associations than by legislatures or kinship. Both seek to overcome forms of individualism that severed the tie between liturgy and community. Both struggle to make worship a means for personal and social formation if not transformation. Both are reaching back to the early church for alternatives to their immediate historical patterns, whether they are the state-supported churches of Europe or the frontier revivals of America.

Both Protestants and Catholics have been greatly affected by the songs and worship practices of African American churches. While the longing for freedom and release that flowered in spirituals can often be sentimentalized, the songs of the civil rights era (and now the powerful songs of the South African liberation movements) brought a deeper appreciation for biblical themes of justice and of the need for new relations between blacks and whites. The U.S. holiday commemorating the birth and life of Martin Luther King Jr. has become for many churches a special Sunday to rehearse the vision for a world in which racial distinctions are not the basis for injustice but for enrichment. Moreover, the kind of spirit, freedom, and vital participation characteristic of most African American worship has been for most European American churches a breath of fresh air in the liturgical skeletons of earlier revivals and preaching movements.

In recent years this infusion of African American elements into other North American churches (with considerable resonance in Europe as well) has been augmented by the spread of Hispanic, American Indian, and Asian songs into the hymnals of these churches. While many congregations still revere their old tunes and lyrics, the presence of options opens up a sense of wider representation in every church and an openness to diversity that did not necessarily exist before. It is this emphasis on diversity, multiculturalism, and full representation that becomes a new set of values shaping worship. Whether sheer diversity in worship is enough will become a theme in my unfolding argument. That it is a powerful ethical theme in worship today cannot be overlooked.

In addition to the value of diversity and ethnic inclusion, we see yet another set of values increasingly informing worship reform—harmony with nature and ecological responsibility. Nature provides the symbols of choice for reformers such as Brian Wren, because it can bring in both the nurturing values espoused by most feminists as well as the pressing claims of ecologists. From this source come both the goddess themes of archaic religion and images from contemporary physics. Where older hymns may have sung of the starry heavens filled with cherubim and seraphim, a contemporary composer writes:

Stars and planets flung in orbit, galaxies that swirl through space,
Power hid within the atom, cells that form an infant's face;
These, O God, in silence praise you; by your wisdom they are made.[4]

Such a hymn then seeks to combine the incomprehensible expanse of galaxies (surely there are other creatures longing for God's salvation out there!) with the classic anthropomorphism of traditional theology. Hear the fourth verse:

Humankind, earth's deepest mystery, born of dust but touched by grace,
Torn apart by tongue and color, yet a single, striving race;
We, in whom you trace your image, add our words to nature's song.

Notice how the ecological and multicultural themes come together within this cosmic perspective. Humanity, made in God's image, is part of creation. Indeed, it must work to catch up with nature's oneness and internal harmony as well as with its union with God.

In one sense, these ecological and cosmic themes present the greatest challenge to the biblical and classical concerns for proper governance, whether that governance be seen as monarchical, republican, or communitarian. Contemporary physics, with its chaos theory, cybernetic and electronic equilibriums, and multicentered universes, offers a rich field of symbols for democratic publics, where mutual influence, multicausality, and random innovation can play important roles. The more difficult ethical question is whether any form of human governance can lead humanity to a better harmony within the natural limits of our planet. What is the connection between governance and ecology? Might not the commands of a dictatorial ecologist be more effective than the interminable contention of a pluralistic democracy? Would archaic spirituality, whether expressed in monarchical or communitarian symbolism, offer some clues to a way ahead, or would it inevitably become yet another form of collective nostalgia unable to engage the questions of justice, human rights, power, and authority?

The ecological question takes us to the widest horizon of ethical factors shaping the reform of worship. These cosmic themes reopen the question of preindustrial and prebiblical religious symbols as a way of healing the alienation between humanity and the rest of creation. One way to get at these connections within traditional Christianity is through a dialogue with Eastern Orthodoxy. In general, the Eastern

Orthodox churches have been more a catalyst of reform in the western churches than an actual participant in reform. The work of Alexander Schmemann, for instance, has been widely helpful as a lever for change that avoids a simple choice between Catholic and Protestant traditions.[5] More recently, however, orthodox theologian Vigen Guroian has probed the ethical ramifications of orthodox worship.[6] Not only does he, along with other orthodox theologians, point out the rich way orthodox traditions shape personal and communal life, but he also indicates areas of necessary change. Guroian sharply points out how the organic communalism implied in most orthodox worship can simply make the church into a traditional cultural enclave rather than an institution dynamically engaged with the cultural and social complexities of American pluralism.[7]

Amid these cultural and social complexities, it is important to note the way reforms in American Jewish worship have become increasingly important for Christian developments. Historically, American Jews have picked up much of the worship patterns of American Protestants, just as the synagogue was tending to become a voluntary congregation of "believers." That is, Judaism had to develop the model of voluntary association typical of American religion—including its worship patterns—if it was to survive and prosper in such a pluralistic society. However, reaction to the Holocaust of World War II caused Christians to begin to reappropriate the ancient Jewish roots of their own worship, especially in connecting the Eucharist to Passover. The ethical question of how Christians ought to relate to Jews began to become an important element in Christian worship, whether as related to how Good Friday is celebrated and interpreted or to how Christians name the parts of the Bible in worship. Should the Old Testament be called the "Hebrew Bible" in worship? How should John's disparaging reference to "the Jews" be read? Should Christians celebrate a Passover seder as part of Holy Week? These questions form yet another set of ethical factors in the reform of Christian worship.

And finally, reforms of worship have had to deal, although largely obliquely, with the problem of "civil religion." Throughout much of European history Christian worship was itself the glue of social cohesion and the cultural foundation for governmental authority. The rituals of court mirrored the rituals of the Christian cult. A hierarchy of mirrored paradigms of order bound believers to their parents, to lords, to kings, to Christ, and to God. With the increasing separation of government from church both in Europe and America, churches were free to develop their own worship patterns according to the needs of somewhat independent congregations. The state and civil associations involved in the political realm had to start developing their own forms of cultic legitimation. In the United States, the Revolution, the presidency inaugurated by George Washington, the sufferings of civil war and Lincoln's martyrdom, not to mention the military exploits of "manifest destiny," all contributed to the development of a civil religion that waffled portentously between defense of the Constitution and civil rights and sheer militaristic jingoism and imperialism. European countries, especially Germany, suffered from the collapse of monarchical orders, the marginalization of traditional religion, and the resurgence of state-supported mythologies that justified enormous atrocities on all sides. In these countries the effort to build up a civil religion to support the new constitutional orders must now contest with the scars and memories of the churches' blind acquiescence to the cultic trappings of Nazism, Fascism, and Communism.

The churches in the United States were likewise swept up in this ambiguous and burgeoning civil religion. Flags appeared in sanctuaries (alongside "Christian" or papal flags), the Fourth of July and Memorial Day became worship events, and songs and hymns to America peppered the hymnals. Here again the kind of worship patterns sought in reform have to take into account the relation of churches to other institutions, not only religious institutions, as with Judaism, but civil institutions as well. How indeed can the church's worship symbolism be critically engaged with the civil themes around it without supinely reinforcing them? That is a question we will return to in the last chapter.

Each of these reform emphases raises crucial ethical claims. Catholic reformers have emphasized the communal grounding of liturgy while Protestants have struggled to recover the full range of their senses within a tradition of the Word read and preached. Both have tried to shape worship to form and hopefully transform persons and societies. In both traditions we see efforts to reclaim both the archaic symbols of maternal nurturing and the futuristic themes of astrophysics and ecological destiny. Themes of liberation and multicultural diversity emerge from the many voices previously silenced by segregation, colonialism, or other forms of ethnic, racial, and gender domination. The interplay between Jewish and Christian worship introduces sensitivities to religious dialogue and interdependence. Finally, the development of civil religions within secularized nation-states challenges the churches to a critical engagement that can speak the language of constitutional republics without simply singing their song.

Each of these ethical claims has an integrity that must be honored. The question I raise here is: How does worship cohere with the struggle for a world where these claims and the people who present them can live together in justice and peace? That is the primary question of integrity this book is trying to address. How, then, should we proceed in order to respond to this question? The first and decisive step is to turn to the classic body of thought about how people govern themselves. It means we need to think about worship using the perspectives of political theory. What does this choice involve?

WORSHIP AND ETHICS: WHAT PARTNER SHOULD WE CHOOSE?

Our selection of a partner discipline for working through theological issues shapes our theological conclusions, often in unrecognized ways. For years theologians have turned to the psychological disciplines as partners for thinking about the work of the church. While primarily informing the way ministers approach pastoral counseling, psychology has also shaped the way they think about administration, leadership, church development, and worship. This partnership between theology and psychology leads us to focus on how worship activity functions in the individual believer and the way the psychological needs and dynamics of that believer are replicated in the symbols and rituals of worship. The familial images of Mary and Jesus, of the Holy Family,

of the sacrifice of the son to fulfill the wishes of the father—all inter-
act powerfully with individuals' own deep experiences and motivations.
Likewise, bloody sacrifice, so repugnant to democratic citizens, powerfully dramatizes the inner struggles people have with feelings of aggression, victimization, shame, guilt, and grandiose victory.

Sigmund Freud's analysis of the mythic structure of the mind and
emotions opened up the "royal road" between the psyche and ritual
symbols. In his *Totem and Taboo, Moses and Monotheism,* and *Civilization and
Its Discontents,* he pointed out the necessary role of symbolic life in sub-
limating inner drives of aggression and sexual longing so they might
empower the social institutions of constraint and cooperation that make
civilized life possible—though often at a great price to the self's need
for internal well-being. Within the Freudian framework, however, the
rituals and symbols of worship were always reduced to their "real meaning" in the dynamics of the individual psyche. In the end, this reduction truncates any effort to talk about worship as the representation of
transpersonal or transhuman realities. It inherently invalidates the worth
and even reality of the church or of a God who encounters humanity
and creation in a real drama of salvation. Nevertheless, it contributed
an indispensable language for talking about the powerful way in which
classic myths, symbols, and rituals function in the emotions and sub-
conscious dynamics of individuals who might otherwise think they
had moved beyond the "superstitions" of religion.

Carl Jung took Freud's theory of symbolic meanings and began to
anchor this personal symbolic world in a wider, transpersonal world of
"collective archetypes." Like the worship traditions that precede and
follow our individual lives, the archetypes link our own inner symbolic
life to a wider world of meaning. The symbols of worship—in whatever religious tradition—have an independent reality that shapes us
and enables us to become participants in a wider culture. The familial
struggles to find a proper relationship with parents, siblings, and children are not simply manifestations of our inner biological drives but
patterns of relationships that make humanity and creation possible as
such. They are part of a shared world, not just the expression of individual needs.

This perspective obviously has more to offer for theologians concerned with worship, since it affirms a transpersonal reality in which worship symbols are embedded. Worship can be seen as playing an indispensable role in human development by providing its own royal road leading people from their individual constructs into a world of shared meanings—the meanings of the worshiping community. Worship enables people to become more fully human. Rather than being simply a projection or a means of psychic constraint, the symbolic and ritual life of communities becomes a way out of the imaginations of the heart and the solipsism of the mind into a more genuine shared social existence.

Moreover, the Jungian program opened the door to a way for Christian worship leaders and theologians to see connections with other religious traditions. They could begin to identify the "primitive" and "pagan" roots of Christian worship. Mary could be seen as an expression of the primordial goddess, and baptism as a way of expressing the universal struggle for individuation. Jungian analysis could help guide liturgists by connecting their worship reforms to the universal paradigms of collective human imagination, thus giving them an intuitive and emotional validity not apparent from the standpoint of ordinary science.

A Jungian approach could enable people to move beyond a strictly individualistic and reductionist approach to worship. It also helped steer people away from a therapeutic approach to worship, in which worship should heal or transform people, and toward a socialization approach, in which worship functioned to move people from their more limited intrapsychic and interpersonal worlds to a wider society. Worship could be seen as formation as well as therapy.

Once people began thinking about the psychology of formation or socialization, they could pick up other psychological theories that concentrate on the mind and behavior. The view of worship as an educational process lies deep in Protestant traditions, with their focus on hearing the Word. In the work of Stanley Hauerwas and John Westerhoff, for instance, worship is a process in which communities form virtues in their members through a kind of learning process that conditions them to certain habits and orientations.[8] Without this ethical education we cannot form stable characters that can sustain trustworthy relationships. Without these virtues, we would not be able to cultivate enduring communities of loyalty and cooperation. To make the connection between the cultivation of virtue and the work of worship, such theologians seize either implicitly or explicitly on a cognitive or behaviorist psychology quite different from the psychoanalytic tradition.

Both the psychoanalytic tradition in therapy and the cognitive and behaviorist traditions embedded in educational psychology lead to questions of community and common life. Both psychological approaches require further expansion in a sociological direction. In order to develop the social implications of the idea of archetypes, psychoanalytic thinkers turned to the work of anthropologists, while cognitivists and behaviorists turned to the idea of community and theories of the public. Both shifts are important for understanding the relation of ethics and worship. Both are needed to move toward a more holistic perspective.

I have already pointed out how the disciplines of cultural anthropology have influenced our current thinking about worship. The primitive rituals that Durkheim, Malinowski, and Evans-Pritchard observed, for instance, can be seen as laboratory models for Christian worship. Because of the relative homogeneity of these primitive models of community, these anthropologists were led to see all societies in terms of their unity. People trained in this tradition tended to ask: How do societies sustain their unity in the face of the actual complexity and pluralism of modern life? How do the parts of the social body function so as to enable the whole to survive?

For classical anthropologists, religion, with its symbols of transcendent unity and rites of inclusion or exclusion, provides the glue for communal unity. Such a perspective makes sense within a relatively homogeneous society, such as we imagine parts of European Christendom to have been. However, when applied to worship in pluralistic societies, this perspective tends to illuminate only the internal workings of congregations or the necessarily emergent "civil religion" of a whole republic.[9] What it does not do is focus on the complex relationships among congregations, denominations, para-church organizations, and other powerful symbolic institutions, such as sports, entertainment, education, and the military—in short, the way most people live.

Similarly, the "community" language many ethicists and theologians use to talk about worship suffers from this unitary image of human society. Working with a community notion, they are often led to emphasize the necessary gap between "the community" and "the world," a gap critics often see as a theological contrast between faithfulness and sin when in fact it may be a gap arising from an inadequate sociological theory. The choice of the language of "community" may simply distort what is involved in complex institutional relationships. To grasp this complex pluralism more adequately, prescient observers such as sociologist Peter Berger turned to economic or political theories as partners for understanding worship.

Early on, Berger turned to the economic theory of markets to trace relations between the cultic life of the churches and their actual social situation.[10] From this perspective worship services became "services" in a market driven by consumer preferences. Churches that could adapt to preferences shaped primarily by entertainment industries, civic and military rituals, or cultural tastes could prosper, while others withered in the rigidity of tradition. When transfigured into questions about the ethics of worship, this economic analysis tended to revolve around questions of psychology. How can worship appeal to the psychological needs and dynamics of individuals and families? How can worship meet the needs of its "consumers"? How can worship better engage their psychological needs as relatively autonomous individuals? Such an approach generally reinforced the relation of churches to the private sphere, as we shall explore later.

When critical questions about capitalism's privatizing effect on worship are raised, apologists for worship generally turn to communitarian values embedded in its ancient traditions. However, this effort to revivify those ancient patterns only tends, as an ethical criticism of capitalism, to awaken dreams of socialism, communalism, or even primitive communism rather than to engage the realities of capitalism in our own time.

More radical economic theories, principally stemming from Marxism, yield ambiguous results for worship. Some theologians, such as the "Slant Group" in Britain in the sixties and seventies, tried to make a case for the need for worship forms that "open up" the realities of class struggle and the need for revolutionary liberation.[11] However, because a Marxist analysis inevitably subordinates culture to the forces of production, worship never can gain enough independent basis to represent transcendent purposes or powers. The symbols of worship must always serve the interests of revolutionary leadership, and are thus denuded of their inherent power. Finally, arguments based on economic determinism fail to account for the ongoing reality of political organization, which is why Marxist regimes could never construct constitutional polities to channel and constrain the struggle for power. While ethics and theology informed by Marxist critiques could prophetically lift up the inequities and savage exploitation of economic life, they could not develop a political theory to help people deal with the broader struggle for power, authority, and meaning.

What is needed in a pluralistic environment is a political theory, that is, a way of thinking about how a pluralistic assembly of people works out its common life within specific geographies, histories, and hopes. Politics is the articulation of the relation between *e pluribus* ("the many") and *unum* ("the one"). To work out this common life, the language of organism and primitive unity that so permeates anthropology and much sociology has to give way to political theories of pluralistic conflict and of constitutional authority, participation, and association.

Political theory deals with questions of power and authority that lie beyond the sphere of friendship, kinship, and relatively homogeneous communities. It is a theory about publics or about matters capable of becoming public. In Richard Sennett's terms, it deals with the way strangers can live together.[12] In Hannah Arendt's view it deals with the realm beyond the private world of face-to-face relationships.[13] Biblically, it begins with Israel's confederation, in which tribes bound by ancestry formed a common alliance, or covenant, in loyalty to a God who transcended kinship, procreation, sex, and name.[14] Such a politics beyond kinship has always needed to appeal to a transcendent source of authority in order to bring warring tribes together in peace. This is the source of the deep connection between worship and politics, the touchstone for biblical worship as well as much of the inheritance of Christianity. Political theory thus forms a critical, perhaps central, partner for thinking about worship.

In shifting from these earlier partners to that of political theory, we can better identify the ethical issues raised by our search for greater integrity in worship. This is a strange and audacious claim for most ears. This shift will not be easy, since it means liturgists, ethicists, and theologians will have to become as versed in political theory as they have been in psychology and anthropology. What, indeed, would such a choice mean for the way we think about worship? To answer this question we need to think more directly about the relation between worship and ethics.

HOW SHOULD ETHICS SHAPE WORSHIP?

Once we have selected political theory as our partner for thinking about worship, we have to ask how we should think about the relation of ethics to worship. The first of two aspects to this question asks how ethics should shape worship. The second asks how worship should shape ethics. I will first deal with the way ethics shapes worship.

The most important way that ethics has been reshaping worship in recent times emerges in the feminist critique of male-dominated language and symbolism. Women either did not exist at all in worship language ("he" always represented "her"), or they appeared only in subordinate roles, even if indispensable and powerful. Mary (and many other female saints) may have been able to manipulate the levers of salvation behind the scenes, but she lacked the crucial element of democratic life—equal citizenship and the capacity to exercise authority equally with men. Identification of the incongruence between the values of democratic citizenship and the forms and language of worship lay at the center of an ethical critique of worship. This appeal to democratic values has then resonated with many other claims for representation from groups hitherto excluded from the church's symbolic life. In the Americas it meant representation for descendants of enslaved African peoples, for aboriginal peoples, and for Asians as well as for people with physical disabilities. Such an appeal can then claim that the faces of the natural world and nonhuman creatures need to find a voice in our worship. Each year, for instance, animals of all sizes and descriptions enter into the Cathedral of St. John the Divine in New York City to be blessed as part of that church's effort to reintegrate all of creation into the sacramental life of the church. In principle, then, worship symbols and rites should include everyone, regardless of biological form and appearance. The whole world becomes a democratic assembly pervaded by the mysterious source of all things.

Worship reforms based on this ethical claim have greatly affected worship language, rites, and even church structures. Gender-inclusive hymnals, lectionaries, Bible translations, prayers, and rituals too numerous to cite here have flooded our bookstores and pew racks. Ordination of women to all church ministries has proceeded steadily though not without obstacles. These changes and challenges have met their strongest resistance in churches with deep and strong liturgical traditions or those rooted in fundamentalist and literalistic scriptural beliefs. For the former, worship stands above and precedes all ethics; it embodies traditions that are self-authenticating and cannot be judged from an independent standpoint. For the latter, worship scarcely exists at all. The individual stands in direct relation to God's Word as revealed in the Bible and has no need of the mediation that occurs in symbolic rituals that inevitably require a priestly functionary.

HOW SHOULD WORSHIP SHAPE ETHICS?

Resistance to such ethical claims by highly liturgical churches raises the question of how worship should shape ethics. There are really two kinds of questions here. The first, represented by official Roman Catholic resistance to feminist liturgical and ecclesiastical reforms, claims that the symbols of worship received from Christian tradition stand above and precede ethical critique.[15] Christian ethics—its norms, values, and fundamental orientations—should be formed by the sacramental models found in the historic liturgies of the church. Thus, the model of male headship exemplified in the Trinity, in Christ's relation to the church, and in God's relation to creation should shape and form Christian ethical reflection. While this is tempered by the strong tradition of natural law in Roman Catholic teaching, such a relation of worship to ethics is seen to prevail at the core of Christian ethics.

The other way the precedence of worship over ethics finds expression is more typical of Anglican positions. While worship should prevail at the core of the way individuals, families, and Christian communities are formed ethically, the forms and symbols of worship itself must be open to prophetic critique. The Anglican ethicists Timothy Sedgwick and Harmon Smith represent this kind of middle road.[16] What is important to note, however, is that the received patterns of worship have a presumptive priority in shaping ethics as well as in cultivating ethical people until confronted with strong arguments from reason, biblical prophetic traditions, or the fruits of the human experience of most Christians.

At some point, of course, the tension between ethical critique—whether from the standpoint of democratic values or biblical prophecy—and received forms of worship and symbolism comes to a standoff. Conceptions of the Trinity are one example. For feminist critics, the trinitarian formula of "Father, Son, and Holy Spirit" is simply a metaphor drawn from patriarchal society to describe the Divine. The structure of authority it undergirds tends to undermine any woman's effort to claim authority in the religious community. Thus, it should be replaced with an appropriate gender-inclusive equivalent, such as "Creator, Redeemer, and Sustainer."[17] Defenders of the patriarchal symbolization claim it is not a mere metaphor but a genuine symbol of the Divine, that it participates in the essence of divinity. Changing the symbol of Father and Son would direct us to some other god. They contend that it is not a metaphor anchored in our own experience and ethical commitments, but a symbol by which the Divine is in some way represented to us. To baptize people with any other formula is to baptize them into a church other than the Christian church, a divine life other than the God of Jesus Christ.

Such a dispute is not amenable to rational resolution, though I will show later how a political analysis can reframe the question in important ways. Christians can only live around the dispute, try to localize its effects, and await the outcome of historical developments. What the dispute helps us understand, however, is that worship symbols are deeply ethical matters. How they are ethical matters is open to quite divergent perspectives that are not only a matter of whether worship shapes ethics, or vice versa, but of the nature of symbols and metaphors and of the relation of persons, groups, associations, institutions, and societies, not to mention the relation of societies to the nonhuman world. To try to get a handle on these questions we need first to arrive at an understanding of how we see worship functioning in the life of faith, both personally and ecclesially. In the next chapter I will seek to clarify our understanding of the purposes of worship. We can then explore how a political reconstruction of worship symbols fits into those purposes.

CHAPTER THREE

Worship as Political Rehearsal

A LL DECISIONS REGARDING WORSHIP are shaped by our understanding of its purpose. People have often stated this purpose in theological terms. Some have held that its purpose is to glorify God. Others emphasize that its purpose is to save souls. Still others hold that it should seek to continue the incarnation of God in Christ, or to reignite the spirit of God among the people. These are not mutually exclusive, of course, but an emphasis on one purpose subordinates the other purposes to it, thus shaping the practical decisions we make about worship. In order to get at the ethical meaning of worship we have to ask this question of purpose in terms of how worship shapes human action. In reflecting on the many efforts at worship reform in recent centuries, I see three different understandings of the purpose of worship at work.

WORSHIP AS EDUCATION, MOTIVATION, AND REPRESENTATION

The first perspective sees worship functioning as *education*. This purpose is deeply embedded in churches originating in the Protestant Reformation. In a world of illiteracy, widespread superstitions, and an often magical understanding of worship, the sixteenth-century reformers in Germany, Switzerland, and the Netherlands focused worship on the exposition of scripture. They developed catechisms to instruct the people and used the sermon as the central point of access into participation in the divine economy. All adornments, gestures, and rituals that might distract from a hearing and understanding of God's Word were stripped from worship. Among divines in England and the United States the sermon became a model of rigorous thinking, exposition, and explanation. Lying behind this enormous development of the sermon as the centerpiece of worship was the belief that right understanding was indispensable to a right response to God. An understanding conformed to God's Word could shape and guide the will to right action. Reason could and should rule the will. Or could it? An awareness of the limits of rational understanding led preachers in the Reformed tradition, such as Jonathan Edwards in New England, or later John Wesley and George Whitefield, to craft sermons that would also move the heart. The test of a sermon's educational impact became its capacity to move the audience to repentance, conversion, and a new way of life. The chief purpose of worship became motivational. It was meant to affect emotion and the heart.

The purpose of worship as personal *motivation* is best represented in the evangelical Social Gospel tradition. Songs, prayers, rituals like baptism and communion, personal testimonies, and above all preaching energize, transform, convert, and empower the participants to work both individually and collectively to resist injustice and create justice in the world around them. The way African American churches empowered the civil rights movement in the 1960s represents this approach most dramatically. Personal, communal, and ecclesial interests all coincided in the drive for civil equality in American public life. The liberation of this relatively unified community could draw on powerful biblical themes of exodus, restoration, resurrection, and Pentecost. To the degree that worship becomes a kind of vivid reenactment of these dramatic themes it leads us to the third perspective, that of worship as representation.

In this perspective, worship is the *representation* of the divine order of things. God, the work of salvation, the life, death, and resurrection of Christ, and the incoming of the Holy Spirit—all of these are represented in worship. Worship mirrors the divine life that orders and redeems creation. Such a view permeates much of Roman Catholic and orthodox traditions. Worship is so richly symbolic precisely because it seeks to make the richness of the divine life available to us. The focus is neither on the participating individuals nor on their task of worldly action but rather on God's action through the worship itself. This usually implies that just as God is eternal and unchanging, so must the liturgy be. God's holy transcendence is then interpreted in terms of unbroken tradition rather than as the basis for the ethical critique of all tradition.

All three of these perspectives clearly have their limits. The educational model forms analytical minds that can clear away the idolatries of unworthy devotions, but it can leave the heart cold and fail to strike sparks at the hearth of human motivations. It can establish the basis for a clear ethical and legal order, but it can also easily lead to a merely judicial understanding of sin, grace, and salvation. The motivational model can certainly mobilize people, but it tends to neglect the way patterns of worship themselves lift up models of future existence as well as reinforce existing patterns of action in families, work, or civil institutions. For example, in the relation of Protestant churches (both black and white) to the civil rights movement, there was little or no discussion either of the issue of gender inequality in church symbols or of the possible contradiction between the monarchical structure of power in many churches and their members' fervent hopes for a fuller democracy.

The representational approach, though providing symbols that evoke hope in a transformed existence, often pays little attention to the actual transformation of individuals or communities, let alone of nonreligious institutions. The crucial point is merely that God's eternal pattern of right order is rehearsed in symbolic ways—ways that over time often become quite distant from the social patterns and symbols in which the church exists. Thus, it falters at the effort to bring the world in line with the eternal paradigms articulated in worship. As Vigen Guroian has pointed out, a church with this kind of worship emphasis can easily become an enclave both insulated from the world and also unfaithful to the very ethical claims it rehearses in worship. The Russian Orthodox Church, for instance, survived the enormous pressures of the Communist era and has emerged once again, often with longings for its old position in Russian society. However, it seems little able to make critical contributions to the reconstruction of Russian society along democratic lines.

In different ways, each perspective rests on certain assumptions about the relation between church, community, and society in order to work out the ethical dimensions of worship. Both the educational and the motivational models, whether in white Social Gospel churches or in the black churches in the civil rights movement, tended to assume that individuals—usually members of the middle class—had the occupations, positions, or social resources to implement the ethical perspectives nurtured in their consciences. They only needed the understanding and the motivation to activate their wills. The black churches could largely assume that opposition to white racism had amalgamated the black church and black community. The only question was the liberation of this single reality to participate in the wider republic, if not, as black nationalists sought, to create its own. The liberal white churches assumed that people could move from pew to boardroom and office in order to implement the social vision taught in the churches.

The representational model usually works with a slightly different assumption about the relation of church and society. It assumes a high degree of congruence between the two, because this model works only if believers are present as a community to the daily and weekly presentation of the images of God's eternal order. That is, church and people must coincide. Such a model of the relation of worship to ethics presses for a national church that is not merely a state church but truly a church of the whole people. As we have seen most recently in the Balkans and to some extent in other Eastern European countries, such a representational model can thus exacerbate rivalry and warfare between people for whom nationhood is rooted in religious legitimation. The tension here is not between monarchical symbols in worship and democratic aspirations in the wider public, but between the divine model of harmony and the actual religious nationalism it often fuels.

WORSHIP AS REHEARSAL OF GOD'S RIGHT ORDER

A fourth perspective is needed that draws on the strengths of these three perspectives but seeks to avoid the limits they evidence in a pluralistic republic serving democratic values. It also must have theological warrant and cultural appropriateness. The line of argument pursued in this book sees worship as the *rehearsal* of God's right order. It recognizes the importance of affirming a divine purpose and ordering, but also the need for our participation in it. It recognizes the importance of learning the "scripts" provided by scriptural heritage, but it knows that we have to enact them dramatically if they are to reshape our lives. Worship as rehearsal affirms the essentially public character of worship as an experience held in common.

The metaphor of drama at work in this perspective also affirms the constructed character of our life as well as of our worship. Psychologically, it draws both on the psychoanalytic sense of symbolic expression and the cognitivist and behaviorist emphasis on repeated reinforcements of actual behaviors. Moreover, it affirms core claims of the humanistic approach by emphasizing the importance of self-actualization in action. This dramatic action schools people's capacity for improvisation, reworking, collaboration, and actual performance. Our virtues are cultivated in the rehearsal of relationships and narratives presented by regular worship themes.

Crucial to the language of rehearsal is its recognition that all worship is ultimately provisional, meaning it awaits the final unfolding of God's purposes. The gap between heaven and earth is the gap between now and not yet. This is the gap in which ethics functions to shape actions grounded in the past but oriented toward a possible new future. As Don Saliers stresses, worship is essentially eschatological, even as it celebrates the presence of the future through its symbolic action.[1]

To spell out this perspective further we need to take a moment to talk about the key words we have been using all along but without explicit definition—metaphor, symbol, ritual, and worship. Theological and liturgical language is filled with metaphors.[2] Metaphors are words or concepts that use a familiar meaning to help us grasp a less familiar or necessarily hidden reality. Metaphors serve as bridges between the known and the unknown. They are also a way for us to transfer emotions and meanings from the familiar reality to the less familiar.

The parental love of God or the cool waters of God's mercy come to mind as metaphorical images rich with emotion and meaning derived from our immediate experience.

Symbols are metaphors or metaphorical constructs that have taken on a life of their own. They are so associated with the reality beyond our immediate experience that they begin to embody it as an experience in itself. In Paul Tillich's words, they begin to "participate in" the reality to which they point.[3] As we saw above, "God the Father" is such a symbol. Substitutions of other metaphors for God are questions not merely of how God "functions" in our life but of God's very "being."

A symbol thus begins to create an experience. It is itself a reality we enter into rather than one we control. When Christians take part in the Lord's Supper, they are not just remembering some past events whose recital would take much longer. They are entering into the very process of redemption that occurs through the drama of Christ's sacrifice on the cross. Whether or not the meal is a "sacrifice" or the present enjoyment of a future heavenly banquet is an important theological question, but what I want to emphasize is how the eucharistic ritual is a symbol of some transcendent reality in which we are able to participate by virtue of this symbolic activity. Indeed, this symbolic reality is so powerful it begins to recreate us in its own image. We begin to conform ourselves to the values, dispositions, themes, and narratives it sets forth.

When we speak of worship as rehearsal, we assume this kind of symbolic character of worship. Like a play, worship is a reality into which we step, taking on another *persona*, lines of another author, with sets and sequences of some other time or no time at all. By putting worship symbols in this dramatic context we affirm their close connection to ritual. Ritual consists of repeated symbolic actions within a prescribed format. Ritual action always involves shared meanings among the participants. That is, it creates a certain kind of drama, albeit one with known conclusions and a fairly fixed set of meanings. Ritual, in short, is a regular dramatic enactment within the symbolic framework of worship.

Worship is the broadest term for this symbolic drama, encompassing the whole arrangement of words, music, arts, movement, space, and dramatic sequence. The word *worship*, of course, indicates that this symbolic action points us toward what is worthy and especially what is worthy of our praise and devotion. That is, it lifts up this symbolic activity as an ethical action that vivifies and inculcates values to direct our lives. It lifts up the values and patterns of right order and goodness that we are to emulate or entertain as fundamental to our lives. It is our paradigm of service. It rehearses the goals, powers, and patterns we are to serve in our life. Thus, we usually speak of "worship service" in one phrase, bringing together the dynamics of "worthing" with those of enactment in "service" of those values or of the God who ordains them. With its emphasis on adoration of a preeminent figure—God— and of service to God, the concept of worship tends to reinforce the classic hierarchical relationship between lord and vassal. In other words, it already contains a decision about proper political order; indeed, it is an order against which I am contending as our proper paradigm for Christian worship. Thus, the term *worship* itself is problematic. Nevertheless, I think we can continue to use it to talk about the general way our ritual activity establishes what is worthy of imitation.

Worship and *liturgy* are closely intertwined terms, especially in this dramatic conception, since liturgy is any one of the "set pieces" in worship. Since it is also rooted in an ancient Greek conception of the "public works" of those who patronized civil festivities, it too is closely connected with service. (Ironically, these ancient "liturgies" were offerings only of the well-to-do, though the literal interpretation of liturgy as "work of the people" has been used in our own time to undergird a democratic conception of worship.) While we often use liturgy and worship interchangeably, I will generally use liturgy to speak of fairly settled ritual parts of worship—praise sequences, confessions, prayers, responsive readings, and the like. They are the more stable conventions of the worship drama—the Lord's Prayer being the most familiar.

Worship is a dramatic action of rehearsal in two senses. First, it is always an activity that only anticipates the final event. It is a preliminary action. It mirrors our own life of faith in which we act in light of the coming final action of God—the "eschaton." In this sense all worship is anticipation. It is symbolization of that which is yet to be. It is not merely a mirroring of an "eternal world overhead" but of a world that is yet to be, even beyond our present categories of time and space, life and death. It is a matter of story more than of idea, of narrative more than of proposition, of creative action rather than imitation of an eternal form. Worship is always a preparatory activity in light of this coming fullness of God's creative work.

As rehearsal, worship is also an enactment of what we already have learned. In this sense it is a matter of memory and memorial, of representing what we already know in a way that trains our speech, motion, and emotion so that the lines and action flow through us. More and more, we become one with the characters and the story. Even with this effort to meld into the received drama, in rehearsal we also try out our own interpretation of the play and the action of our character. We reshape the drama. We begin to participate in authoring the story anew. To be sure, some actors perform with more "authority" than others, and they are usually set aside officially as the priests and ministers of the worshiping assembly. Because they know the drama so intimately and have entered into its spirit so deeply, they are able to recast it without losing its underlying ethos, direction, and power.

Such authoritative acting only occurs when it is also received by the audience, whether in dress rehearsal or in full performance. This is another characteristic of rehearsal—the presence of sufficient audience committed to and capable of helping us act out our lines and character. Theirs is a critical but also supportive presence, encouraging us toward the best. It readies us for the wider public of strangers who come to share the drama with us. The drama creates a public of shared meanings, enabling strangers to relate to each other. It becomes a world of shared reference, as the plays of Shakespeare have become for English speakers and those of Goethe for German speakers.

This is yet another link between the idea of rehearsal and that of worship—they are public activities. They press for public life even as they create publics. The interaction of characters with each other and with audiences constitutes a public world that transcends them as individuals. Drama, worship, and public life are intertwined realities; they all share in this work of creating a public life together. Just as church and "ecclesia," the ancient Greek public assembly, are related, so is worship and public drama. All are involved in creating and sustaining a public realm enabling people to enter a world of meanings they could not construct or vivify on their own. The cult of ritual actions in worship cultivates a peculiar public in which people gain a new and peculiar identity. The identity and story they live out in worship then presses to be the story and character they live out in every aspect of their lives. At this point the cult of formal worship begins to become the culture underlying their common life.

Worship is a dramatic activity that can and usually does seek to develop a more general culture. Worship is cultural foundation and cultural action. It builds up a world of meanings, conventions, reference points, scenarios, and characters that become the elements of a full life. Over time the boundary between the ecclesial cult and a people's culture can blur and dissolve, as with our examples from the experiences of orthodoxy. The experiences of New England Congregationalists or Southern Baptists tell similar stories. Whether blurred or sustained in distinct tension, this movement from cult to culture (and from culture back to cult) can develop the foundations of a public life—or at least some of its crucial ingredients. It develops the root values and agreements as well as the sense of history, character types, and proper relationships that enable strangers to share in a common enterprise. That is, the cult-culture matrix begins to form the basis for legitimating other institutions in that culture's public life.

As many sociologists have pointed out, all politics, government, and public life depend on this shared cultural base. Without it, political authority lacks legitimation. It cannot appeal back to shared commitments and values in order to elicit cooperation and voluntary compliance. Politics depends on culture and culture depends on vibrant cult. This is the root assumption behind inquiries into the nature of "civil religion," the identification of the cultic base for seemingly secular political cultures. Without the cultural life fostered by this cultic base, politics soon descends into coercion, violence, and a warfare of all against all. The world constructed in the rehearsals of worship can ultimately make possible a realm of political freedom based on persuasion, nonviolence, and shared purposes.

Our exploration of the meaning of worship as rehearsal of God's right order has led us not only to a particular conception of worship but also of the relation of worship to public life. This perspective on the relation of worship and ethics, which may be unfamiliar to many people, sees worship as the bridge between theology and ethics, and ecclesiology as the bridge between Christian ethics and general public life. All of these elements—the church, worship, and public life—are held together by the idea of drama. Drama itself emerges from the very human capacity for public life, for appearing before others in roles that are parts of a larger drama. The church's worship, as a rehearsal of God's ultimate public, sets forth a kind of "proto-public" in which people can express themselves in song and art, confess their life in sin and health, praise that which is worthy, and long for the perfection of their life together.

So far, I have worked out this conception of worship in terms of the movement from cult to culture and public life. At this point we need to work back from this conception of worship to its specifically theological basis. Worship is the rehearsal of God's right order, but what do these last three words mean? There are three sources for explicating the meaning of this phrase—biblical religion, the historic experience of the church, and the nature of human beings as seekers of perfect publicity.

Within biblical religion, the assemblies of Israel and of the early followers of Jesus as the Messiah saw worship preeminently as the public expression of longing for and anticipation of God's governance of their lives. In their worship they remembered the gracious acts by which they were originally constituted in covenant, Exodus, Torah, and now in the crucifixion of Jesus, his resurrection as Christ, and the pouring out of his spirit at Pentecost. At the heart of their worship they rehearsed their hope for the full realization of God's governance to come in the near future. As distinct from many contemporary understandings of worship as a private matter directed at personal therapy, individual conversion, accumulation of members, or the preservation of a "community," their worship was rehearsal of this anticipated new order of justice and peace—the new creation.

God's new governance would entail a renewal of the whole creation. The fulfillment of God's covenant with Israel would include the flourishing of the earth. In the words of Isaiah, rehearsed again in John's Revelation:

> For behold, I create new heavens and a new earth; and the former things shall not be remembered or come into mind. But be glad and rejoice forever in that which I create; for behold I create Jerusalem a rejoicing, and her people a joy. (Isaiah 65:17–25; cf. Revelation 21:1–2)

Right order, then, means above all a structure of justice that ensures wholeness of life among human beings and the land. The city represents this image of structured justice shared by a people who live together. It is an "order" not in the rigid sense of a fixed conformity but in the sense of a trustworthy relationship between God, the people, and the whole creation. It is "right" in the sense that it is congruent with God's purposes for the flourishing of creation, not merely as a system but also in terms of the ends of each of its creatures—something we can scarcely comprehend but can only anticipate with faith.

This longing for Israel's right order often used the symbols of David's monarchy to grasp and proclaim the significance of the resurrected Jesus as the inaugurator of this perfect order of justice and peace. It was Jesus' challenge to the precarious balance of power and authority in Palestine that brought about his crucifixion as "King of the Jews." The model prayer he taught his disciples began with the petition that God's "kingdom come on earth as it is in heaven." What is important to recognize at this point is not which political symbols framed this hope but that the hope of Jesus and his meaning for the church as the Messiah was specifically a political hope—a hope for the right governance of the world.

This hope has resonated throughout Christian history, often with bloody and catastrophic results. Images of the Crusades vie with reflections on the church's preservation of much of classical culture and civilization. The work of worldly unification struggles with the bloody conquest of the Americas under the sign of the cross. In short, the image of God's right order is buried in our history as a contorted body of tragic aspiration. While the tragic character of this hope has often driven sensitive and devoted Christians to try to purge their faith and worship of political symbols, we cannot do so without eviscerating both our biblical heritage and our liturgical and ecclesial memory. Moreover, we deprive ourselves of the awareness that the achievement of justice and peace requires a structure of authority and power that can curb our sin and coordinate our gifts. The question is what political language and form should such an aspiration for a just order take. That is the question driving these reflections on worship, which is the way we envision and symbolize this ultimate order.

Finally, such a political orientation to worship rests on a particular way of seeing human beings—a theological anthropology. That is, people are seen as creatures struggling for a wider public appearance and confirmation. From a theological standpoint they are created in the divine image. This means they are struggling to participate in the divine glory, power, and authority. They are struggling to participate in the trustworthy relationships rooted in the divine source of all life. In a word, they are struggling for a perfect "publicity" in which they know and are known in a field of mutual confirmation. The kind of public confirmation we fleetingly experience in public life, in its tabloid tawdriness as well as in truly moving public dramas, is but an anticipation of such a perfect publication of our lives. "Going public" is both an awesome and often terrifying experience. Worship ought to be the dramatic rehearsal of such a hoped-for perfection of our lives. This is the kind of human nature it should presuppose as it dramatizes its connection with the transcendent source and goal of life. This perspective on human beings should also shape the kind of psychology we work out in connection with worship. It can help us draw links between the necessary private work of therapy and counseling and the wider participatory life of the church.

In my earlier book, *God's Federal Republic,* I laid out these developments and perspectives in greater detail. For the purposes of this essay

I only can point out that the republican revolutions of the last two hundred years, fueled by both Western humanist and Christian and Jewish traditions, have produced the dominant language of political order today. Even dictators want to be known as presidents chosen in popular elections. Even tyrannies seek to clothe themselves in constitutions. Even totalitarian party–run states want to be known as "democratic republics." This is the language of legitimacy. It is also the language of political hope and aspiration for the sake of which millions have died in this century. This, I would argue, should be as much the language of worship today as kingship was in ancient times.

While this may be a compelling ethical and theological claim, it does not seem to have played a role in worship in the last two hundred years. Partly this is because many people thought of worship only in motivational terms. Partly it is because people thought representations in worship should reflect tradition rather than prophetic anticipation. In order to link a political theory of worship to actual practice, at least in most North Atlantic churches, we need to understand better why worship in the forms of monarchy and patriarchy has survived so long in the midst of a world longing for more perfect republics, greater democracy, and constitutional orders grounded in fundamental human rights. That is the question we need to explore in the next chapter.

CHAPTER FOUR

Sunday Monarchists
and Monday Citizens

"THY KINGDOM COME . . ." we solemnly intone in prayers, liturgies, and hymns, and yet in many of our churches a memorial plaque commemorates all those who sacrificed their lives to preserve and extend democracy and republican order around the world. Such a split between the symbols of worship and those of political justice occurs neither in the Bible nor in most of church history. It is a recent split, traceable in part to ideas of "separation of church and state," but only partly explainable with this formula. We are all familiar with the reasons for separating the institutions of religion and government, but here we are dealing with a kind of symbolic schizophrenia. What does this split consciousness mean? Why has it endured so long in our faith and worship? How has it functioned? What does its persistence say to our efforts to construct a coherent language and symbolism that engages our heritage of faith as well as our strongest ethical commitments?

To begin to answer these questions, we need to remember how these democratic commitments emerged, what they have meant, and how they have contested the symbols of monarchy and patriarchy deep within our religious traditions. While the struggle for democratic and republican forms of governance reaches back to ancient villages, councils, and cities, it was the American Revolution of 1776–83 and the subsequent U.S. Constitution that launched the modern forms of this aspiration. Classic republicans sought to create public orders in which interested parties could argue within a constitutional framework of law to achieve their common purposes. Their democratic comrades sought to ensure the widest possible participation in those publics without regard for any biological, cultural, or physical criteria. Typically, republics with democratic values tried to establish federal structures to enable small publics to participate within larger frameworks of common law, authority, and power. Constitutional systems have been developed to allocate authority not only among states, regions, and central governments but among the various functions of government. The purpose of this federal differentiation of power and authority is to prevent a centralization of power that would overwhelm the capacity of people to govern themselves through rational debate among relative equals. These terms—*republic, democracy, constitution,* and *federalism*—constitute the core language of legitimation for our common life on this planet. They do not spell out specific content for particular peoples, but they do shape our dominant images of political justice and political hope.

The past two centuries have witnessed enormous conflicts over the proper economic and cultural basis for such participatory governance. Is republican life best supported by a socialist, a capitalist, or a cooperative-based economic order? How can democracies be ecologically responsible? What conceptions of human rights need to undergird widespread participation in public life, regardless of our biological constitution or particular achievements? How should these republican forms engage the racial, ethnic, familial, and religious bonds that shape people's lives? These pivotal questions consume a great deal of our time, energy, resources, and even our very lives.[1]

The question for Christian worshipers is this: If such a longing and language is so powerful and pervasive, why has it not begun to permeate the language of our worship? Why does the drama of our worship still rehearse the world of feudal and ancient monarchy? To be sure, women as well as men, not to mention people of many cultures and complexions, increasingly populate this symbolic world of worship, but this move toward inclusivity has only incidentally changed the way we envision the structure of right political order that frames our hope. Why are we monarchists on Sunday morning and democratic citizens the rest of the week? Why do we pray for coming kingdoms when we sacrifice our lives for democracies and federal republics?

When I have asked these questions both among professional theologians and among church members generally, I have often been met with highly emotional responses. Some say that only such archaic symbols can guarantee the awe and wonder necessary to God's transcendence. Others claim we worship precisely in order to enter an archaic world that anchors us in the midst of the almost intolerable strains of social change, a world that provides comfort and stability. The irrelevance of feudal and monarchical symbols makes them available for a life of utopian and even dangerous fantasies. Still others claim that to abandon such symbolism would rob us of most of our music, prayer, and even architecture. Changes in worship must be organic, they claim, and such proposals ask for a whole new garden—a utopian impossibility.

The high emotion of such responses indicates that complex and fundamental issues are at stake here. Analyzing these issues can help us understand not only what blocks a shift in political metaphors and symbols in worship but also how worship relates to ethics and public life. To grasp these tensions we need to probe even more deeply into our religious history.

POLITICAL FORMS IN BIBLICAL EXPERIENCE

The clash of political symbolism between monarchy and republic originates in Israel's ancient life. Fundamentally, there were two symbolic and political traditions—a divinely constituted monarchy rooted in David's court in Jerusalem and a conciliar federation rooted in God's Torah given at Mount Sinai and celebrated with the traveling ark of the covenant at Shechem and Shiloh. The ritual of Torah worship with a traveling ark legitimated a "federal" relationship among the tribes. Indeed, our word *federal* is simply derived from the Latin *foedus,* the word for covenant. Covenants were originally the intertribal, interkingdom treaties relating suzerains to vassals and binding allies to one another. Thus, Torah, covenant, councils, and decentralization of both worship and governance all went together. Indeed, the book of I Samuel claims that Israel adopted kingship only in violation of its heritage.

True worship of Yahweh meant decentralized governance according to a common Torah, a devotion we mirror today in our obedience to written constitutions.

Kingship, however, was the usual way of the nations, especially in order to centralize power for the sake of warfare. It found its brief but definitive manifestation in the reign of David, who centralized cult and court in Jerusalem. In addition to the military security offered by monarchy, two additional factors seem to have embossed this image of right order on Israel's faith and hope. First was the sheer cultic weight of the Psalms, even if only a few of them actually arose in his court. God's covenant with Israel was reinterpreted as a treaty relation between Yahweh and David's line. God's covenant, rather than legitimating the rule of Torah law through councils of elders, became the basis for a monarchical dynasty. The throne on earth became a metaphor for God's power and authority, and David's throne became a symbol of divine authority just as Solomon's temple became a symbol of God's presence. Second, the trauma of exile and the renewed vitality of return from Babylonia focused on the rebuilding of the temple with the hope of restoring the monarchy associated with it. Only then could Israel repristinate itself in Canaan.

What is important to see is that though the general notion of "God's right order" can be seen behind both the federal and monarchical languages of this anticipation, Israel's worship had to speak one of these specific tongues. Israel's worship is not a philosophical discourse bound up with general propositions about God. It is an ensemble of liturgical conventions cast within a dramatic narrative that knows a specific story of God's grace in founding, preserving, and ultimately saving the people who live by God's strength ("Israel"). Praises issued forth to Yahweh, King of Zion, or to Yahweh's Torah. Psalm 93, for instance, places Yahweh firmly within the frame of monarchy:

> The LORD [Yahweh] reigns; he is robed in majesty; the LORD is robed, he is girded with strength. Yea, the world is established, it shall never be moved; thy throne is established from of old; thou art from everlasting.

Indeed, Israel's God judges within a council evidently drawn from Babylonian models:

> God has taken his place in the divine council; in the midst of the gods he holds judgment. (Psalm 82:1)

The language of monarchy found throughout the Psalms was of course oriented to David's court, either in actuality or in exilic and postexilic memory.[2] As with Psalm 110, the Davidic monarchy became a kind of mirror of the heavenly right order of God, though to be sure in a clearly subordinate fashion.

> The LORD [Yahweh] says to my Lord, "Sit at my right hand, till I make your enemies your footstool."

Thus, this language of governance became not only a metaphor for God's right order but, with the Psalms and then with the prophecies of Isaiah, a symbol of that anticipated order. It was this symbolization of the future, eschatological government of God that came to constitute the language for understanding Jesus as the Messiah who inaugurates that new order. Jesus, the crucified rabbi, became Christ the King in order that the assembly gathered around him might speak a widely held language anticipating God's right order of governance. This symbolization has dominated our understanding of Jesus as Christ ever since.

Matthew and Luke rehearsed Jesus' supposed Davidic ancestry and located his birth in Bethlehem in order to place him in the Davidic line (even though Joseph was not his biological father by their account). The Psalms and prophecies of Isaiah frame many of his crucial acts— his reception and baptism by John (Luke 3:4–6, Matthew 3:3); the announcement of his mission at Nazareth (Luke 4:16–22, cf. Matthew 4:12–17); his claim of authority (Luke 20:41–44, Matthew 22:41–46); and his crucifixion (Luke 23:46, Matthew 27:46) being only a few. Regardless of what Jesus may have taught, the Davidic title, with its penetrating critique of this world's power and authority, finally claimed his significance for the early church. And though Jesus spurned the title of

king, Pilate's mockery on the cross determined the world's image of
him.

THE CHURCH, MONARCHY, AND CHRISTENDOM

The worship of the early ecclesia focused on the representation of
Christ's Passover meal. With thanks (*eucharistie*) for Jesus' sacrifice for
their sakes, members of the early assembly uttered intense prayers in
anticipation of the coming new order breaking in on them and inaugurated with Christ's resurrection and ascension, and with the pentecostal
outpouring of the Holy Spirit. The disciples of Jesus prayed "Your
kingdom come" and concluded (in the Aramaic tongue of Jesus) with
the word *Maranatha*, "Our Lord, Come" (1 Corinthians 16:22).

In spite of the almost archaic monarchical language in which this
worship was framed, the early assembly also remembered many elements of Israel's conciliar tradition. In the church of John's Gospel,
Jesus was known as Logos as well as King. He was seen as the basis for
the speechlike reality that organizes the world and enables people to
relate to one another in persuasion and fidelity rather than conquest
and command. He was the preeminent "logic" of the new assembly of
peace. Or, as with Paul, he was the wisdom of God, a peculiar upside-
down wisdom of self-giving that began with the knowledge of a crucified God rather than a victorious king. Moreover, the ritual of immersion (baptism) into this wisdom of God made of each believer in the
assembly a participant in this new order of righteousness. Baptism's
bestowal of citizenship in the power of the spirit of God already began to dissolve the worldly hierarchies of power and authority.

Democratic and conciliar elements notwithstanding, the cult of
Christ continued to speak a dominantly monarchical language, not only
because of the Psalm heritage of Israel and the prophecies of Isaiah
but because that was the governance language the wider world could
understand. In the postrepublican Roman Empire of emperors and
kings, this was the only language of hope for perfect governance that
people knew. On apologetic grounds alone this would be the song and
speech of Christian worship, even if Christians spoke of a transcen-

dent God of a new creation instead of the mortal monarchs of their world.

The teachings of Paul also exercised a decisive impact on the way early Christians understood the way Christ mediated this divine new order. Paul's emphasis on the problem of individual sin, guilt, and forgiveness began the slow process of turning Christian faith from an expectation of perfect governance to a hope for personal release from guilt and anxiety. Largely cut off from the Palestinian context of Jesus' preaching and ministry, Paul focused on how people might have a new birth through participation in the cult of Christ. Baptism was no longer purification in anticipation of the coming reign of God, as it was for John and presumably for Jesus, but rather a burial into the body of Christ so that one might participate in his resurrection power, overcoming sin, guilt, and death. Baptism into the body meant baptism into the presence of Christ in the eucharistic meal and in the Christian assembly. While the eschatological hope persisted in a general form (Romans 8:19–24, 2 Thessalonians 1:5–2:12), it was increasingly swallowed up by a personal hope for resurrection and immortality (1 Corinthians 15). This reduction of a collective futurism into individual psychology courses through Augustine and on to the later Middle Ages and the Protestant reformers.

From the standpoint of the original political eschatology of the church and its scriptures, it is not at all a surprise that the emperor Constantine adopted this Christian cult as the basis for his own imperial order. Rather than being a fall from this cult, Constantine's appropriation was, in this respect, its natural outcome. This perspective radically challenges the usual negative view of the Constantinian revolution set forth by the conciliar tradition, which focuses on the work of the Holy Spirit, or the pietist tradition, which sees Jesus as an apolitical figure. In fact, while Jesus may have been diametrically opposed to the ways of governance around him, he lived in the fervent hope that God's right order of governance would prevail and indeed was prevailing in his life. Constantine merely usurped this monarchical mantle of political hope, adorning it with the symbols of his own particular regime and collapsing the distance between his own empire and God's order.

In the influential words of Eusebius, Constantine's enthusiastic biographer, Constantine "frames his earthly government according to the pattern of that Divine original, feeling strength in its conformity to the monarchy of God."[3]

Thus, for good or ill, the Constantinian era of Christendom continued for fifteen hundred years in Europe as an experiment in the relation between earthly and heavenly kingdoms. The argument of justice spoke the language of monarchy, and monarchy rested usually in the cradle of male descent. The cult of Christ the King infused the culture of Christian kingship, providing mirrors for princes to emulate and symbols legitimating the thrones of righteous kings and the overthrow of the unrighteous. Subsequently, the French kings laid claim to Davidic ancestry by placing themselves on elaborate Jesse trees in stained glass and murals. Finally, the claims of James I to mirror this divine monarchy lit a fire that engulfed England in a generation of civil war and the promulgation of republican ideas that shaped the modern world.

THE REPUBLICAN REVOLUTIONS

This republican moment was not without its own preparation. Over the centuries, themes of conciliar federation, governance by God's law, and even outright anarchy kept sprouting from the underground roots of scripture and Christian reflection, feeding monastic movements, "heresies," and finally the conciliar movements of the fourteenth and fifteenth centuries. While the church had come to arrange itself around a papal monarchy emulating the princes of the world, these councils proclaimed their superiority over popes and priests. It was this conciliar spirit, at first reserved for clerics and then extended to church members in general, that poured out into Reformation synods, assemblies, congregations, and councils. A renewed reading of scripture reintroduced covenantal ideas of governance into Christian discourse, leading to congregations founded on covenant rather than princely patronage. The radical effort to reserve baptism to adult believers reinforced ideals of citizenship rather than infantile subjection to authority, and the opening up of the full Eucharist to believers on a more regular basis reinforced ideals of democratic participation. Congealing with the reawakening of republican ideals from the ancient Greek and Roman world, this conciliar spirit of covenantal assembly began to form the cultural base for emerging republics and democratic associations.

To undermine the legitimation of Christian monarchy and avoid the religious wars of Christendom, the American republican experiment severed the institutional tie between governmental power and religious authority. The U.S. Constitution would rest solely on the public agreements of the people, and Christian worship would affect them only indirectly by cultivating the visions and virtues of the Christian population. Henceforth the political eschatology of Christian worship, with its monarchical symbolization, would gradually become a private matter of personal conscience, congregational worship, and family life. The churches could retain their symbolic monarchies in worship as long as they did not seek to fashion the public order in the image of their monarchical devotion.

This privatization of worship in exchange for political peace could draw on the psychologization of monarchy already presaged by St. Paul's and Augustine's search for a means of self-control anchored in Christ's rule in our hearts (Romans 13:12–14). What was to be governed by the kingship of Christ was first one's own passions and wayward impulses. As the well-loved gospel song puts it:

> Take my will and make it thine;
> It shall be no longer mine.
> Take my heart, it is thine own;
> It shall be thy royal throne.[4]

Such individual self-control was good for republican order as well as for the political accommodation between the churches and government. The internal monarchy of self-control cultivated the disciplined citizens necessary for a public life of honesty, reasonable debate, and persuasion. The covenant between God and nations was transmuted into the personal relationship of faith and fidelity between each believer and

God. The covenantal habits cultivated in each person's relationship with God could then be translated into the predisposition to make and keep promises in business contracts as well as legal constitutions.

Such devotion was a matter of the hearth as well as of the heart. The psychologization of monarchical symbolism found nurture and expression in the bourgeois Christian image of the Christian home. Emerging in the nineteenth century, the Christian home was a structural expression of the patriarchal and monarchical order rehearsed in worship. It was in appearance a male-headed pyramid of authority disciplining the emotions of women and children just as Christ's headship of the male was supposed to discipline his passions. At the same time, because most men's power was being removed from the home to seek its way in market and mill, women actually exercised the power of the home. Like Mary in the medieval church, women pulled the strings that kept this little church going—creating, sustaining, and redeeming it. Church and home became the realm of monarchy in a world governed by republican constitutions and market contracts.[5]

This, of course, was the emerging ideal for white American Protestants. Biblical themes of exodus still reverberated through the worship life of the children of enslaved Africans seeking liberation from the Egypt of slavery and segregation. While this often became individualized as well, the thrust of collective aspirations always lay near the surface. At the same time, images of conquest and of the realization of biblical political promises flowed into American visions of empire and manifest destiny—forces that always threatened to overturn the fragile republic for the sake of military order and victory. In both cases, however, securing the dream of democratic participation or the victory of the United States' model of republican government always pressed people to privatize the monarchical themes of traditional worship.

The most obvious symbolic expression of this accommodation was the rise of Christmas as the most celebrated Christian festival of the year. With Handel's rendition of the Messianic monarchical hope ringing in our ears, we celebrate the birth of a son who will ascend the throne of God's kingdom and rule in our hearts forever. That an infant son can already be hailed as king can only occur in a world of inherited monarchy. In his glow, even the wise men of Matthew's Gospel become kings in popular song. For all of this, it is still a festival of intimacy and the private life. It is a feast of family, home, and marketplace.

THE FEMINIST CHALLENGE

This accommodation between a religiously inspired private world of monarchy and a public world of democratic self-governance managed to remain relatively intact for more than a century. It was the feminist revolution after World War II that exposed its contradiction and set in motion the challenge to worship that we struggle with here. In 1920, women had finally gained full political participation in the United States with the nineteenth amendment to the Constitution. The logic of democratic public life had finally reached the private realm. Since then, through increasingly equal access to education, work, military service, and political election, women have extended further the range of democratic public values. The simultaneous movements toward full civil rights for ethnic groups in many countries could leave the symbolism of Christian monarchy relatively intact, but the change in women's status exercised the decisive critical challenge to the church, both symbolically and structurally.

It is impossible to review the manifold ways that the feminist movement has reshaped both Christian worship and church order. Where men have prevailed in symbols and positions women now press for an equal role. Father language now coexists with mother; references to daughters and children supplant references to the son. The son who was a crown prince simply becomes a child in a warm and intimate family. What is crucial for the concerns of this book is the almost total lack of attention to the political theory at stake in this change. Deft innovations alter the language of hymns and prayers to place women where men had dwelled alone, but the change of political symbolism is restricted merely to quarrying gender-neutral words from the monarchical world. *Lord*, where it is even seen as a governance term, is replaced by *sovereign*, and *kingdom* with *realm* and *reign*—all of them typical monarchical terms. Why has the feminist critique fallen short of this structural awareness even when the rise of women to public equality depended on the success of republican democracy?

The main reason I can adduce to explain this myopia is that most feminists opposed patriarchy because in the day-to-day struggles for equality men were pitted against women. Moreover, because the wheels of government had been totally controlled by men, feminists sought not merely to replace them but to oppose all forms of political authority as antifeminist. The feminist revolution would bring an end to political authority altogether—an ancient anarchic dream indeed. The struggle between alternative political forms was of little moment in such a view.[6] In addition, it could probably be argued that women, having been deprived of the experiences of public life and politics, simply didn't speak such a language and may even have felt it was against their "nature" to do so. The world of household, family, nurture, and intimacy was not merely the cultural experience of women, it was seen as part of their biological inheritance. The feminist revolution would eliminate the need for political authority altogether, replacing monarchy and governance with nurture and nature.[7]

The shift from governance to love and nurture then opens us up to images of nature and ecology, as in some of Brian Wren's work. Ecology is not only a field of daily economic constraints; it is also a source of symbols for the ultimate ordering of our life. It provides us with deeply emotional symbols even as it opens up the possibility for thinking about organization in terms of intertwining systems of influence held in a delicate balance rather than the simple hierarchies of power and authority typical of the classic monarchical pyramid.

The reintroduction of these natural symbols as well as the full symbolic presence of all peoples and creatures in powerful worship offsets the historic centrality of patriarchal symbols. It does not, however, resolve the persistent question of political order raised both by biblical tradition and human experience. If we are not merely to replace a male with a female monarchy (or white with black, north with south), we must address the question of which vision of governance actually makes possible the partnership of men and women in the care of our world. What form of power and authority can enable warring tribes to share in a common life of persuasion and respect? What is the shape and character of the new order of power and authority into which we are seeking liberation? Which language shall we use to symbolize the eschatological hope of Christian faith? To answer these questions we must clarify the political and theological principles that need to underlie this transformation of worship from its monarchical frame to a world of republics seeking democratic participation and federal relationships.

CHAPTER FIVE

Choosing the Political Imagery of Our Worship

IN THE CENTRAL TRADITIONS of Judaism and Christianity, worship rehearses the governance of God. It gives thanks for God's gift of ethical teachings by which, in Solomon's words, "to discern and administer justice" (1 Kings 3:9). It rejoices in the source of this ordering of our relationships with all of creation. It seeks to extend this justice to others in intercession, and anticipates the coming perfection of this governorship in and through God. This is the focus of John's baptismal work of anticipation of God's new order. It constitutes the core of Jesus' ensuing ministry and forms the astonishing imagery of the revelation with which Christians close their scriptural canon.

Our first challenge is to recover this foundational principle of worship within a society that has reduced worship to individual experience and domestic psychology. Worship has to move beyond being simply a motivational battery for individuals to being the rehearsal of paradigms of a just and creative order rooted in God. It must be the way the faithful assembly articulates its grounding in the divine purpose to draw all people into a perfect public of power, persuasion, and peace.

Our second challenge is to reground worship politically in a way that respects the necessary tension and difference between the actual operations of political power and authority and the transcendent visions rehearsed in worship. Just as Nathan stood over against David in critical judgment, so must Christian worship be distinct both from government and from the civic culture that seeks to legitimate it. Not only must this worship exemplify the critique of Nathan, it must have the transcendent distance expressed by Jesus' claim that "my kingdom

.is not from [or "of"] this world" (John 18:36). The ultimate order of governance rests within a new creation that has burst the bondage of fear, anxiety, and greed gripping our present existence in a fist of mistrust and coercion.

Our third challenge is to imagine a worship that can speak to our present political convictions and aspirations without being swallowed up by them. We need to move from a language of kingdoms to republics, from monarchs to presidents, and reigns to constitutions. This is obviously no simple or easy task. Cultural and religious changes take centuries to run their course. Our emotional constitutions are subtly shaped in family, school, and entertainment media as much as in church. Nevertheless, we must make a beginning. My effort here is truly a search for initial handholds and vantage points for the long and difficult climb ahead.

Such a movement requires concepts and principles in order to develop coherent worship practices. In this chapter I will lay out the basic concepts of governance that I think must underlie such an endeavor. First we need to clarify what we mean by the concept of a republic, with its attendant ideas of democracy and federalism. In the next chapter I will set forth some principles for reconstructing worship within this framework of governance metaphors.

PUBLICS, REPUBLICS, AND THE ECCLESIA

Republic is just one of the most common terms used to refer to the generally recognized legitimate order of power and authority in our world. *Democracy* and *commonwealth* also have distinguished pedigrees. I have placed *republic* at the center of this constellation of terms for several reasons. First, it articulates a principle of political order, as distinguished from democracy, which at its core only deals with the principle of participation. Republics are grounded in publics, that is, assemblies of people who come together not because of their biological similarities or kinship but because of a desire to live together and share a common land. They are united by a sense of justice expressed in love rather than a sense of honor rooted in loyalties to families or individuals. This is what inevitably moved republics to sever their ties with kingship, whose principle is descent rather than public deliberation. Either the king is descended from earlier kings, or, if elected, is seen to be "kin" of the people. That is, kingship is a principle of ethnicity rather than publicity, of blood rather than oath and pledge; it is a household writ large, in which the ruler is the parent of the people. This is why queens can fit its frame so easily. It is also why love and nurture can be confused so thoroughly with justice and governance.

Although Matthew and Luke saw Jesus through monarchical eyes, the actual experience of the early followers of his way was quite different. The early church, with its struggle to transcend familial and ethnic ties, saw itself first as an "assembly" (*ekklesia*) rooted in a common faith, hope, and mutual care. Its pentecostal origins broke through the alienation of linguistic diversity without obliterating the uniqueness of each tongue. That is, the church's origins are rooted in a fundamental political need to form a common discourse in order to engage in the practices of persuasion. The longing for an even more perfect public than the ones we ordinarily experience is tied inherently to the church's source in the pentecostal mystery of shared understanding and discourse. The church is a peculiar public that anticipates an unimaginable perfection.

A public is not merely a congregation of people, but of people "locked in argument about their common good," to use John Courtney Murray's phrase.[1] They are not merely registering their opinions in secret, whether electronically or in voting booths. They are arguing with each other, seeking to persuade each other, and struggling in conversations to identify the right questions and press for greater understanding and mutual agreement. A public is composed of people speaking with each other about matters they have in common. Their speech is not only about the land and wealth they already share but about the possible futures they might have together. At this point we see the pertinence of the term *commonwealth*, which should be seen in its broadest sense of "common weal," or all those things that make for wholeness and health in a common life. It is the matters of the commonwealth that a public argues about. Unfortunately, the term tends to imply that it is their common economy that binds the members together, more like merchants in a large association than citizens with equal rights to participation in an assembly. Nevertheless, commonwealth remains an important and indispensable member of this symbolic framework, though not the central one.

A public demands not only the presence of a sense of commonwealth but also of a citizenry with public virtues. By virtues I mean the classic notion of the strengths necessary for public life. The ancients saw them as courage, temperance, prudence, and justice. These strengths were later often juxtaposed with and even seen as opposed to the "theological" virtues of love, hope, and faith. The concept of God's republic helps us to see their proper relationship more clearly. Both are necessary to understand our participation in present publics and in the fullness of God's republic yet to come.

The courage to participate in public requires little rehearsals in trusting circles of friends before our entrance into the larger company of strangers. In these little publics, indeed little theaters, we seek to express who we are in a way that will find resonant confirmation. In this sense, the church is not only an anticipatory public but also a "proto-public," generating new publics around it. Much of who we are arises in the interaction between the roles we take on in these little performances and our own rendition of them. As narrative theologians have held, we gain our own unique persona in history through playing the roles of others who have gone before us. Our courage grows as we live into the roles of our heroes and heroines. Gradually we are enabled to move to a fuller profession of who we are as a participant in the central drama of our historical communities. The assembly of Christians ought to help people enter into the widest possible drama of God's saving intention for creation. Thus, the courage to participate in the dramas of our lives is shaped by our rehearsal of the life of a fuller republic of resonance and confirmation for which we hope in faith.

Publics are also arenas with a disconcerting variety of people. Every public not only is built on a plurality of participants but also fosters greater pluralism as people share opinions, judgments, and perspectives. In the work of a public, people are invited if not constrained to transmute their necessary differences, based in biology and origin, into differences that can be argued for the sake of mutual accommodation.

A public seeks to lead people beyond the differences they cannot change to live a life together based on the ways they can agree to live with and through their differences.

The capacity to engage this plurality in such a public way demands self-restraint and moderation as well as a prudential sense for the appropriate actions to take in complex situations. These classic virtues of temperance and prudence are critical in a life of persuasion that respects other citizens as well as the limits of one's own power and perceptions. They are not unrelated, then, to what some people call public friendship or public love. Here the love extolled in the Scriptures is linked to the conditions not of intimacy but of public life, life in the assembly, the congregation of God's people. This is in part the meaning of the word *charity*, which needs to be rescued from reduction to sheer benevolence and restored to its place as a description of right relationship among equals.

Publics, in order to remain worlds of persuasion, require the development of a rough equality among the participants. Equality, a value usually attached to the field of democratic ideas, is in this world of meanings not a mechanical or mathematical identity among the participants. It is not a matter of their having identical strength, but rather it points to a quality of participation in the life of persuasion. That is, it flows from the kinds of relationships people have in a public. For persuasion to occur there must be some rough equality of strengths— economic, intellectual, and coercive. But the primary purpose of this rough equality is not to secure the isolation of each from the other in a condition of private defensiveness. It is to enable them to enter into a public life of persuasion and relationships grounded in consent concerning their common good.

A public, or republic, as we call the full political realization of public life, is characterized by such participation, plurality, equality, and persuasion. It has connections to democratic ideas of equality and of a common weal. But none of these principles or activities can exist for long without the presence of some sense of common bonds, connections, and purposes. I have already sketched out the way some of the classical virtues of public life can be related to the theological virtues

flowing from participation in the assembly that longs for the completion of God's purposes for creation. However, we still need to identify
the way the relationships among the participants and among the publics they inhabit can be better grounded. In order for people to argue
out their agreements they have to have things in common. In shaping a
republican vision we have to deal with the need for some commonality,
which can enable us to engage in the life of public argument, persuasion, cooperation, and mutual care. In the worlds of biblical assembly
and of subsequent republican life, this role has usually been played by
the idea of covenant.

PUBLICS NEED COVENANTS

Worship infused with anticipation of God's republic ineluctably leads
us to the symbol of covenant and its political expression in federalism.
Covenant as a concept of relationship stands in contrast to biologi-
cally grounded notions of family, kinship, tribe, and race. While the
two are sometimes intertwined in its biblical origins, it is covenant that
first provides a principle of human organization beyond kinship. Covenant is rooted in promise rather than paternity. Covenant, originally
referring to the treaties among the powers of the ancient world, emerged
as the primary metaphor for understanding the relationships among
Israel's tribes as well as of their relation to a source of order that transcended the ties of ancestry and descent. While the abiding power of
kinship almost swallowed up this principle of promise, Israel managed
to steer away from a sense of kinship with the Divine. The people of
Israel were not sons of Yahweh but servants or partners in promise. If
anything, in those patriarchal days, they were "sons of the covenant"
(*b'nai b'rith*). They were not descended from God, but chosen and elected
by the Holy One. They stood in a relation of political promise rather
than biological necessity.[2]

The peculiar relation of freedom and obligation in covenantal relationships can be seen in the presence of two crucial aspects of biblical
covenant. On the one hand, covenant is simply offered by God to the
people as a presupposition of their existence. The people can refuse to

enter into this covenant, but they are not really free to change it. It comes down "from above" like the surrender terms offered by a suzerain to a potential vassal. Moses' reception of the Ten Commandments on Mount Sinai is its archetypal expression. On the other hand, even in the biblical account, God's covenant with Israel is also the product of negotiation, including, I might add, Moses' clever chastisement and shaming of Yahweh to prevent Yahweh's destruction of Israel for its idolatry at Sinai (Exod. 32:11–14). We have two different readings of this covenant in Exodus 20 and Deuteronomy 5, not to mention its elaboration in Leviticus. Covenant is also the solemn agreement among outright equals, like the covenant between Jonathan and David. Covenant-making thus has two aspects. It is both presupposed (and thus imposed on the present generation) as well as negotiated among contemporaries.

Covenant's implicit mutuality is rooted in its promissory character. Both sides subscribe to it. This idea of covenant is further democratized, if you will, in John's presentation of Jesus' statement to his disciples that they should know themselves not merely as servants but as friends (John 15:15). Covenant provides a world of political freedom rooted in persuasion and promise as well as a world of cultural presuppositions rooted in received covenants. It is a framework of consent rather than of coercion. This concept of covenant is most familiar to us as constitutionalism. Constitutions are something we receive from founders of our republics, but they are also continually renegotiated through amendments and legal interpretation.

This covenantal relation of promise in Israel's establishment meant that the drama of its existence was not so much the cycles of nature and natural necessity but of keeping promises, of anticipation of fulfillment of promises and memory of the trust that emerges with the keeping of promises. It is also lament, confession, and repentance in the breaking of promises. The idea of covenant thus underlies Israel's dramatic sense of history as promise-making, promise-keeping, promise-breaking, and promise-restoring.

Covenant provides the frame not only of historic drama but of mutual obligation. The promises of God and of Israel constituted the

instruction in relationship that came to be called the Ten Commandments as well as the rules of life for those in covenant, both ritually and
socially. This covenantal framework served as the reference point for
Israel's arguments about justice and goodness. This covenant was rehearsed in ritual recitations of God's gracious calling and liberation of
these tribes. It shaped and formed the virtues of justice that had to
permeate their behavior and disposition if they were to be true to the
kind of God who rescued them from slavery. Covenant provides the
fourth classical virtue of public life—justice—but does so within a
framework of fidelity to God, the Covenanter. It unites the virtues of
justice and faith. It was only in confidence of God's faithful protection
of Israel that the citizens of Israel could be freed to pursue justice with
one another and with the stranger in their midst. The collapse of justice in Israel was always connected to Israel's loss of faith in God and
its anxious, fearful desire to protect itself through coercion rather than
righteousness and fidelity.

Biblical covenant was not only tied to the rehearsal of right relationships among the people but between them and the land. First of all,
this land was a place of habitation for the people. It created boundaries
of peace—the purpose of the book of Numbers. That these boundaries of peace have also been the basis for brutal warfare over the centuries is part of the burden of our own sin that we bear in the tragedies
of history. The divine intention was peace and human well-being. But
there is even more that leads us from a concept of covenant that simply
defines our rights as a particular people to a particular space. God's
covenant-making also entails the care of land as a part of creation.
There is an inextricable link between the keeping of covenant and the
care as well as keeping of the land, not merely to advance our own self-
interest but also to affirm it as an expression of God's creative goodness. Creation itself is a participant in God's covenant, not only with
Israel but with all of humanity. Without this ecological move, covenant
can be reduced to the legitimization of our own special claims to a
piece of land rather than the divine call to share the land with all of
creation. Today we can recognize that the covenantal heritage draws us
to a mutual relationship with all of creation. The other creatures of

our natural world are also in some sense participants in this divinely rooted covenant. This is the ecological moment in covenantal life. This "world-house" is literally the ground of our common weal as well as history's theater. Covenant is bound to creation as well as to our own longing for the perfection of our life together.

COVENANT CRADLES CONSTITUTIONAL FEDERALISM

Finally, covenant leads us ineluctably to two crucial political themes— constitution and federalism—both of which are indebted to the covenantal tradition. Covenant forms a kind of symbolic bridge between religious traditions of ethics and worship and the political language of our time. Constitutions in the republican world are the modern manifestation of covenantal promise-making. As written documents, like the Pentateuch itself, they establish the basic agreements by which a people seek to govern themselves. They define the conditions of membership, of the allocation of powers and authority, and the procedures for selecting and limiting leadership and representation. While they arise from the arguments of the people's public assemblies, they also seek and need to transcend them if they are to become the stable world of reference for the ongoing governance of the people. They are both presupposed and also negotiated in the course of their history. They are not rooted merely in the spirit of the ancestors but in the spirit of the present generation.

Thus, covenant is seen as the foundation of law in the sense that it provides the basic set of trustworthy expectations by which a people might create and engage in public life. Without such law we are reduced to caprice and coercion. We cannot trust one another other than the way an infant might trust a mighty parent (a frequent metaphor for our relation to God within traditional monarchical culture). Israel is called to trust in this law to secure its freedom, which is why it is seen as such a gracious gift of liberation. Thus, Israel saw the Torah as its true king. Even today Torah scrolls receive a crown in Jewish worship to remind people of the supremacy of God's law. In the seventeenth century English Puritans such as Samuel Rutherford countered the claims of monarchy with the slogan "Lex, Rex" ("The law is king").

Unfortunately, Christians in the Latin West have tended to see this law through the eyes of Paul and Augustine. Whether or not they understand them correctly, they have come to see "law" simply as the bringer of guilt, fear, and anxiety. It is seen in its psychological impact on perfectionist personalities rather than as the political basis for a free republic. This psychologization of law and the covenantal thought behind it has thus reinforced a conception of worship as the therapeutic care of individuals rather than as the rehearsal of the covenantal grace that makes possible a free public assembly.

Covenantal thought and practice not only underlie the constitutions that make public life possible, they also inform the tradition of federalism by which republics might be linked together in common cause. Publics generally have to be fairly small in order to make possible widespread participation, face-to-face persuasion and agreements, and shared liturgies of grateful remembrance and hopeful anticipation. In order to preserve the crucial characteristics of public assembly and the power of cooperation among publics, republican tradition has turned to the principles of federalism to knit together publics. The alternative to federal relationships has been empire or ceaseless warfare among lesser principalities. Empire is the monarchical principle for large-scale coordination of kingdoms. Federalism is the principle of coordination for republics.

Federalism quite simply is a system of compacts and treaties for enabling relatively independent publics to function as a unity for certain purposes. This set of compacts is itself a constitution for their common life. Each federation, being the product of promise-making in particular historical circumstances, is slightly different. Many of the contests of our time revolve around the nature of the federal relationships that should shape the relationships of the republics of our world. We see this struggle in the U.S. Civil War as well as in contemporary struggles in the new South Africa, the Russian federation, the Republic of India, and in the failed federalism of the former Yugoslavia. Issues of federalism stand at the center of the major arguments over right governance in our time. They are part of the grammar of political hope that should inform any worship seeking to anticipate the coming of God's right order of governance.

Public and covenant form the basic foundations for the structural image of God's right order. They shape the language of "covenantal publicity," by which we can articulate our longing for this new creation of justice and peace. *Covenantal publicity* is simply a general term I use to talk about activities that seek to form publics rooted in and linked by covenants of various kinds. On the one hand, our efforts to build public life ("publicity") require covenantal relationships. On the other hand, our covenants demand the kind of freedom that arises in assemblies and councils of participation, persuasion, and promise.

THE CONCEPT OF GOVERNANCE

For our third component of this republican language we turn to the concept of governance itself. In this case, governance occurs through communication processes central to the life of public deliberation. In our own time we use the idea of cybernetics to express the governance implications of communication. "Cybernetics" is derived from *kybernetes,* the Greek word for helmsman, which the ancient Greeks used to talk about the principle of leadership in their assemblies. It helps us think about the work of governance through presiding in processes of communication rather than through rule or domination over subjects.

In monarchical eras leadership and governance have usually found expression in worship in terms of devotion to a person—the Messiah, the Prince of Peace, and Christ the King among them. In kingship systems right order is bound to personal bonds between master and servant, lord and vassal. Governance, which occurs through a network of personal loyalty sealed in oaths, is a system of personal covenants. Indeed, our very word *sacrament* simply meant in classical Latin the oath taken by soldiers to obey their superiors. This idea of sacramental oath has found expression in worship through practices of kneeling, the laying on of hands, bowing, and clasping hands together in prayer, all of which were ritual elements of oath-taking between rulers and subjects. Governance in the church, which finds its liturgical expression in ordination, simply took up these feudal patterns. The "pastoral" relationships of oversight, direction, and obedience became institutional versions of personal rule. Even today the pope, the most obvious manifestation of hierarchical rule among the Christian churches, takes his name from "papa." He is above all a father to the church family.

This pattern of ritual and organizational personal rule was always challenged by the subordinate tradition of governance by law and teaching, rooted in biblical Torah and Roman law. God's rule was not simply mirrored in the hierarchy of princes, as Eusebius said of Constantine's imperial order, but in the relation of believers to the internalized law of God. Republican governance arises in this tradition—"the rule of law rather than men." With the rise of republican democratic orders and their focus on government according to law, the images of personal rule became privatized. The "personal" bond between believers and God, between the children of God and their heavenly Father, became one of psychological intimacy rather than feudal governance. Instead of bowing before an awe-inspiring sovereign, Christians found themselves singing about walking alone with Jesus in the garden. The liturgies of personal rule that once legitimated governance became a mirror for marriage, family, friendship, and the home.

Christians have generally lacked, however, a liturgy for celebrating God's law. Jews have had the festival of Simchat Torah, in which they celebrate the giving of the Torah to Israel. In the festival of Shavuot they celebrate it as the revelation of God. Protestants have frequently arranged their worship to focus on the Bible, but more as a rule book for individuals rather than as the gracious covenant of God's governance for a people. When Protestants have tried to make these governance connections in the United States, they have tended to turn biblical faith into a support for nationalism or global hegemony rather than a longing for God's governance for the whole creation. Thus, the American flag and patriotic rituals became a part of many American Christians' worship. The more critical approach to the relation of faith and governance espoused either by the Social Gospel movement or by the "neo-orthodoxy" advanced by Reinhold Niebuhr and others has tended to ignore worship altogether, assuming that it is only a motivational matter rather than a rehearsal of God's governance.

The resulting privatization of worship symbolism, either to integrate individuals into an overriding nationalism, to motivate them to social action, or to enable them to suffer the ambiguities of history, has made it difficult to relate worship to the struggle for a covenanted public life. Instead it has tended to draw people away from the field of governance into the intimate relations of "persons." Indeed, the history of the word *person* reflects this move from governance to intimacy. Originally, a *persona* was the mask worn by actors in order to participate in public drama. Likewise, in order to appear in a court of law, people had to have a public *persona*. Latin theologians such as Tertullian then extended this idea of a public mask to the Trinity. God's "personae" were the ways God was present and active in the drama of salvation. To be a person was to be a public actor in history. While such a conception was attacked because it might imply that God's inner reality was different from God's action in history, the notion of God's existence in three persons remained. Over the centuries, this "personality" of God gradually was conveyed to individuals, largely because they took on God's person in Christ through baptism. In the last two centuries it came to mean the unique creative character of each individual, especially in his or her private worlds of intimacy. Thus, to worship a "personal" God means for most people to worship an intimate God rather than a God who participates in a cosmic public and legal drama. The retrieval of God as person in its original sense means a recovery of worship and theology as articulations of the ultimate order of governance—a long and arduous process indeed.[3]

We thus have two problems in symbolizing this steering aspect of governance. The first revolves around the difficulty of moving from a focus on individual rulers to governance through law. The second involves the symbolization of administrators of this law. Let us turn to each in turn.

Governance as Steering by the Mind of Christ

Because of this historic theological opposition between law and gospel, not to mention the frequent corruption of lawyers themselves, we need to draw on other vocabulary to symbolize the rich meanings of

God's law. The tradition of Wisdom, which finds expression in notions of Christ as the logos, and of the spirit and mind of Christ, offer
ways of grasping this original meaning. Much recent interest in wisdom literature has been promoted by feminists because wisdom was
traditionally personified as a woman, the consort of God, the indispensable womb of creation. Through her all things are created. Indeed,
in this respect, Jesus as the logos is the feminine expression of God.
What is of even more interest here is not her gender but her role in
governance, which is why she is associated so deeply with Solomon's
court. In that world, to govern justly is to rule according to Wisdom.
Wisdom entails an administration of justice that takes into account
the complex system of relationships in culture, technology, ecology,
and politics. In cybernetic terms, wisdom is the software of existence—
the basic program for governance.

It is the task of worship to rehearse our participation in the wisdom of God. This is not merely a matter of cultivating the virtues I
focused on earlier in this chapter; it is a matter of engaging all our
senses so that we are attuned to appropriating our world in manifold
ways, aware of the mystery of creation's complexity. It is also a matter of learning how worship can unfold among a people not by commands from a leader but by a collective sense of what to do next.
This "common sense" is gained not only through an artful intuition
but by reasonable discourse—the root idea in logos. This is what it is
to be governed by the "mind of Christ." Such governance, of course,
requires a deep immersion in the culture of the worshipers. It arises
because people come to share a vision, a set of ideals and values, and
a comprehensive orientation to their world and to the historic drama
in which they participate. This kind of leadership and governance
has inspired recent management theorists of corporate culture. From
their perspective, leaders function best when they cultivate a corporate culture that can guide members of the organization without
immediate control "from above."

A recovery of governance in terms of wisdom, mind, spirit, and
logos can help us represent the idea of law as the means by which God
seeks to govern creation. This can be augmented by renewed sensitivity

to teaching and learning as the art of grasping whole information, not just bits. Teaching here picks up the original idea of Torah as "teaching." The divine ordering of our lives is not merely a matter of obedience but of dialogue with God, in which our circumstance is drawn gradually into coherence with divine purpose. With the art of teaching comes that of listening. Through silence, music, and the use of non-musical sound, we can be trained to listen in more sensitive and nuanced ways.

All of this recovery of law and wisdom helps reshape our understanding of being governed by "constitution" rather than personal command. Through the richness of worship we constitute ourselves as citizens of God's republic, living according to divine wisdom. This does not mean that the Bible is in any simple or literal sense our constitution. Rather, it is the crystallization of the founding dialogues and deliberations of the Christian and Jewish publics that have continued to this day. Our governance through constitution is thus intimately connected to our governance through council—another key republican concept. Just as Yahweh was present to Israel in the assembly gathered around recitation of the Torah, so Christians know God as present in the assembly governed according to "the Spirit and Mind of Christ." The church is the assembly where Christ presides. These assemblies, whether gathered from local communities or from the far reaches of the globe, are the popular basis for the church. How these councils of the people are to be understood and structured is the fundamental task of ecclesiology. What is important for our purposes here is to recognize that this gathering, assembling, conferencing, and counciling makes possible the dialogues that continually reconstitute the church.[4]

Council and constitution need to find richer symbolization in worship. Moreover, we need to recognize the importance of liturgy in these assemblies, especially to renew the covenants by which they seek to live. The worship of large assemblies of strangers often has much greater power for us than the familiar gatherings of friends and families that take place weekly in local churches. Precisely because of their truly public character they have a power and authority that often can redefine, indeed reconstitute, us.

The Offices of Governance

Finally, we come to the symbolization of the offices of governance.
How do we symbolize the "persons" (in the public sense) who administer, lead, inspire, teach, and judge? What are our contemporary ana-
logues for the kings, princes, lords, judges, and sovereigns of monarchical culture? The figure of presidency stands at the center of this
symbolic field. In one sense presidents are to councils what monarchs
have been to kingdoms. But their behavior is legitimated according to
different values and principles. Therefore, we must first guard against
the temptation of simply replacing the word *king* with that of *president*.
This simply monarchizes our conception of presidency—a dangerous
enough tendency in our own world. While we need to jar our ears open
by referring to God in Christ as our President, we also need to dig
behind the term to evoke wider symbolic meanings.

People often refer to worship leaders as presiders. They are presidents of the assembly, not in the sense of commanders and rulers but
as conveners and coordinators of the worship according to its constitution (to draw on our earlier discussion). By using the verbal form,
presider, we focus on the kind of action we are talking about. (We also,
unfortunately, distance it somewhat from its strict political meaning.)
Presidency is a function within a constitutional order, not a sovereign
above it. This is why the language of sovereignty to avoid gender exclu-
siveness is misplaced when attached to persons. Thus, when we invoke
Christ to "preside" in our assembly, we ask Christ to preside through
the work of the Holy Spirit that animates our dialogue.

The task of presidency is not merely coordination or parliamentary
monitoring. To preside effectively we must seek to draw in and encourage everyone to give voice to his or her opinions and judgment. An
effective president of an assembly is able to bring participants back to
their primary purposes, visions, covenants, and missions. The president serves the assembly's constitution not in the sense of obeying its
laws but of helping the assembly pursue its vision and be accountable
to its underlying values and purposes. Thus, presidency involves inspiration, persuasion, and exemplary sacrifice for the sake of the

constitution's ultimate aims. In this sense, a true president comes to embody somewhat both the constitution and the people covenanted through it. Thus, some republics, like Germany and India, separate the office of president from the daily maneuverings of parliament, precisely in order to focus on these functions. Moreover, the remaining kings and queens in functioning republics, like England, work best when they serve these functions rather than serve as vestiges of a besieged and corrupted aristocracy.

This work of presidency can also be seen in the historic term *episkopos*, or bishop. The *episkopos* was an overseer, a monitor, a supervisor. While the conception of the bishop's office was often separated from the presidency of councils and transformed into a monarchical mold, its ancient import, when cast in terms of presidency, helps us grasp some of these wider meanings. In this religious reworking of the idea of presidency we can already see some of the reciprocal relationships between political order and worship that we will explore later. The churches ought not only take up the language of republican democracy and federalism, they should recast it in terms of their own theological reflection so they can provide in their worship a mirror of judgment for the practices and aspirations of the republics around them.

While many other elements of the language of republican governance deserve our reflection, I shall conclude this section with only one—election. Election is both richly biblical and political: God "elected" Israel to be a people, and we elect presidents and representatives for fixed terms. A republican turn in worship symbolism would introduce not merely the language of constitution, council, and presidency but that of election. How then can we speak of election with regard to God? It would seem especially offensive to speak of our "electing" the Creator of the Universe. Obviously, the idea of election, like that of presidency, would need some reworking.

We can begin by noting that kingship poses symbolic problems equally difficult as democratic election with regard to God or Christ. Since the time of the Psalms we, both Jews and then Christians, have spoken of God in monarchical terms—the Hallelujah Chorus being only its most egregious expression in our worship. Yet kings were either elected by councils (Saul, for instance), were descended from kings themselves (Solomon), or took their thrones by force. Yet surely, in some strict sense, the Holy One is neither chosen by us nor descended from a parent. Nor does the Creator rule humans by sheer coercion and necessity. In the last case, rule by coercion would either eliminate the meaning of the idea of sin or imply that the one good God causes sin—the classic dilemma of theodicies ancient and modern. Thus, we see that kingship language for God is decidedly metaphorical, though we often cling to it as a veritable symbol of the Divine.

Similarly, while election needs to be seen only as a metaphor, it is a revealing one. The first step is to realize that the idea of divinity in ancient Israel is above all political—it is a matter of electing one's principle of governance. Ancient Israel knew there were many gods. The god Yahweh asked for Israel's decision to follow him. Israel saw itself as elected by Yahweh but also called to elect Yahweh as its god. Similarly, much later, for Christians this god, whom Israel had come to equate with the Creator of the universe and of all nations, was willing to sacrifice himself in the form of his "son" (the metaphorical model nearly implodes here) in order to elicit the faith of the people. In the Pauline theology, which knows nothing of the birth of Jesus as a dynastic heir, God "elects" or "adopts" Jesus to be the Messiah. Likewise, all peoples are called to choose this Messiah as the center of their loyalty. In this political sense, which stands at the core of the tradition, we do indeed elect our God. Election is a reciprocal process constructed in covenantal mutuality.

Election therefore is always related both to call and to covenant. God calls us to elect the divine way, pleading, persuading, hounding, and sacrificing to this end. In the process of this mutual election we are drawn into covenant with the Divine. We choose, commit, pledge, and promise to pursue this particular pattern of relationship with the Divine. We enter into covenant.

Similar dynamics, we might add, occur in presidential elections, especially in the United States and other "presidential systems." Election is a process in which we try to set forth an image of who we are as a people. What are our central values? What vision are we seeking to follow? What are our gods? Such symbolic concerns easily override the pragmatic functions of governance. That is because election is not merely the selection of individuals to perform services, it is also a statement about the covenants and callings that define our common existence. So it is with our election of God.

We have now explored some of the key features of republican democratic order in light of our desire to renovate worship so that it speaks once again in a political tongue that can engage our actual practices and commitments. Central to this field of concepts and symbols are those of publicity and covenant. Covenantal publicity emerges in councils and constitutions where the work of presidency is crucial. Each of these terms can be seen to engage not only our received traditions but our present political practices in ways that alter our understanding of both. Our present worship is thus shaped not only by religious tradition but by political theory and practice. Awareness of this double dialogue with tradition and politics propels us back to the question of how we see the relation of worship to ethics, especially political ethics. Some of the implications of this political symbolism for worship have already entered our conversation. We turn now to elucidation of some principles that might guide us in the reconstruction of worship in light of these issues of governance.

CHAPTER SIX

Some Guiding Principles for Regenerating Worship

W E HAVE NOW SURVEYED SOME of the governance symbolism and language that worship ought to cultivate if it is to be a re-hearsal of God's right order of relationships. The phrase "God's right order" can be interpreted in various ways. I cannot resolve all the ambiguities here. Indeed, much of the ambiguity is necessary if worship is to have a flexible openness to God's activity among us and to our tangled efforts to respond to God's purposes. At a minimum, the phrase must mean worship is always an apprehension and enactment of our proper relationship with God, an envisioning of how God seeks to establish an ever-renewed covenant with us. Preeminently, worship rehearses our participation in relationships of governance, where power and author-ity both sustain and constrain our common life. For the medieval Latin mass, this was a relationship secured in God's sacrifice of his son for our sakes and our accepting this relationship with penitent hearts. The crucifix was its archetypal symbol. For a pentecostal assembly today, right relationship involves the reception of the new spirit of freedom and love that is poured out in our hearts in rivers of emotional ecstasy. For the heirs of New England Puritans, it is a relationship of students to the great moral structure of the universe and especially to the Teacher from Nazareth who both exemplified and proclaimed this enduring order of justice. In each pattern of worship we rehearse a deep para-digm of ultimate right order.

Throughout history, Christians have perceived and rehearsed this divine right order in various ways. The dominant form, of course, was that of patriarchal monarchy. Today a long-struggling subordinate strand of biblical and church tradition has gained expression in the broad tapestry of civil republics and ecclesial assemblies. I have named this activity of governance "covenantal publicity." This is a pattern of human relationships that draws on ideas and practices of assembly and covenant rooted both in biblical and classical humanist traditions. The paradigm of governance that emerges from this activity sees God's right order in terms of some kind of federal republicanism. It is an order of popular constitutions and democratic participation. It is this vision that seeks to regenerate worship as the rehearsal of God's coming republic. Worship in the language of covenantal publicity is a rehearsal of our movement from the privation of fear and isolation into a publicity of trust and confirmation. It is a rehearsal of the constitution of care and cooperation made possible by a God of covenantal power.

Such a move, coming in the face of ancient traditions, is not easy or simple. The point is certainly not to overturn every tradition, practice, and symbol in Christian worship; it is only to generate and recover appropriate symbolism for this vision of God's right order. As with the earlier symbol of the kingdom of God, it functions as a benchmark for the use of other symbolism in Christian worship. Like the gender transformation invoked by feminist theologians, this governance transformation deals with a fundamental perspective in worship without exhausting our symbolic resources. The questions before us are: What principles should guide us in such a transforming effort? How do we honor both the vision that needs to be introduced into our worship as well as the existing dynamics of prayer, ritual, song, and movement? To elaborate these principles we must deal both with values flowing from this vision of governance and with pertinent issues they provoke about worship in general. The first three principles I will present flow from the vision, the last four from the dynamics of worship in general.

Participatory Assembly

Our first principle is that worship must be the work of a participatory assembly. As Harmon Smith points out in his book *Where Two or Three Are Gathered*, the gathering of people into an assembly, an ecclesia, is the first mark of the church and of worship. It is an act of publicity, which in some circumstances marks one for death and persecution. For many people, simply showing up in public takes enormous courage. Because of their life experience they find it almost impossible to trust that they will be sustained among strangers. All of our actual worship excludes as well as includes, not merely on theological grounds but on grounds of class, race, culture, education, ancestry, sexual orientation, and political persuasion. All our worship partakes of the broken and anticipatory history in which we find ourselves. The point here is that our worship should keep inviting, persuading, and pressing us to ever-greater publicity.

It is not enough, however, that we simply show up. Inclusivity is essential but not sufficient. We are also called to enter into the spirit animating the assembly and make an offering of ourselves. For some it is as simple as placing cash in the offering plate, for others it means reading, singing, praying, witnessing, eating, and drinking. It means passing the peace with a blessing rather than a murmur. For still others it means preaching and presiding. The point here is that if baptism means anything, it means seizing our citizenship in God's republic. It means leaving the private world of family and entering the wider public of strangers. Everyone ought to have some access to participation in the presidency of Christ's spirit in the assembly. That is, they should be enabled to help the spirit and mind of Christ preside in the assembly. They should be able in some way to help Christ be represented in their midst.

In this way the assembly rehearsing participation in God's republic becomes a kind of "proto-public" in the society. It is a special kind of nuclear public, a seminary for publicity that nourishes people's capacity for wider publicity. If faithful to the expansive freedom of God's republic it will challenge the limited publics of our world. Indeed, it will threaten them deeply and risk bringing persecution upon it. It is in being this peculiar proto-public that the church makes its most decisive cultural impact.

Sometimes, when the assembly becomes too large, we start dividing it into performers and audience. Then either the performers are seen as representing Christ, or else we get preoccupied with finding ways that the diversity of the audience can be represented in the worship leadership. Both of these accommodations start leading us away from the primary point of full participation in the relationships grounded in our baptism into God's republic. This does not mean larger assemblies cannot rehearse crucial dimensions of the model of God's republic— its expansiveness, diversity, awesome scope, and aesthetic splendor. However, there are real perils and losses here, just as in the small assembly we can begin to cut off the openness to strangers, reject the wider reason of public discourse, and spurn the challenge to go beyond the comfortable horizons of familiar faces and routines.

Just as in any public, an exclusive stress in worship on equal participation can begin to erode the common frame of meaning that gives shape and structure to that participation. If everyone's contribution is equal to everyone else's, we can soon enter into a meaningless cafeteria of mediocrity that fails to rehearse a coherent vision. At this point, we must invoke the second principle to guide us.

COVENANT RENEWAL

Worship must be grounded in covenant renewal. Israel's worship originated in the celebration and renewal of God's covenant with them, first with the traveling ark of the covenant and then in the Temple in Jerusalem. God's steadfast fidelity to the covenant, Israel's constant backsliding, God's persistent acts of redemption, and Israel's joy in God's forgiveness were crucial components of this worship life. Likewise, the assembly gathered around Jesus as the living inaugurator of the new age rehearsed the renewal of God's covenant with them through him. In their thanksgiving meals they remembered his self-sacrificial life and resurrection as the proper paradigm of God's covenantal work. This kind of covenantal memory and hope must find renewed expression in our own rehearsal of God's coming republic.

To do this our worship must first remember the way covenant brings together the source of all creation with the people who seek to secure relationships of trust, care, and peace with all the peoples of the earth.

Moreover, it must bind them together in the promise of mutual flourishing, bringing together God, people, and the land they are to share. Our worship must enable us to rehearse this circle of mutuality rooted in the covenantal tradition.

As Joseph Allen has pointed out in his helpful study of covenantal ethics, we live in a multiplicity of covenants, some general and some particular and special.[1] The promissory web of existence includes not only the universal covenant of God with the entire creation but also the special covenants of marriage, family, work, community, city, and nation. Our worship can be a time when we can order and honor these special covenants within the frame of God's covenant with us. All of them can mediate as well as sabotage our citizenship in God's ultimate and universal public. How we approach them in worship is thus a critical and complex matter, only some of which we can explore in the next chapter.

Our rehearsal of the ultimate promises of God and of a perfect public without fear or betrayal always reveals how far short of this ideal we fall. In classic terms, it reveals our sin in numerous and painful ways. Therefore, our worship is always an anticipation. It is an act of hope as well as of judgment. This awareness leads us to our third principle.

ESCHATOLOGICAL ANTICIPATION

Worship must remember within an eschatological framework. Our symbolic life is both a retrieval of our deepest common memories as well as an anticipation of the future perfection of our world. It is both archaic and anticipatory. Indeed, the more a memory is clouded in an unspecified past the more it can become a symbol for an uncharted future. The glimpses of Eden can become the vision of heaven. Much of our ordinary worship is driven by this archaic sensibility. If something actually happened in the past, no matter how mythological, then it can happen again in the future. Of course, much of this sense of the archaic often dwindles to nostalgia for the familiar past of our own limited histories. Tradition becomes the practices of our grandparents.

A truncated past begins to yield a future of immediate projects rather than of unforeseen possibilities. Authentic worship, however, presses us to our destinies as well as back to our origins.

Above all, however, Christian worship must be eschatological in its orientation. Even in the midst of the thanksgiving for Jesus' self-sacrificing inauguration of a new order we pray for the fulfillment of that new creation yet to come. In remembering his acts of persuasion, moral judgment, healing, and public proclamation we anticipate what makes possible the perfection of our public life. Even with the memory of the worst sufferings of human history, we still rehearse the patterns of right relationship that eventually overcome evil. Without this rehearsal of such promises the burden of the past reduces us to fear, revenge, and hopelessness. It prevents us from apprehending new beginnings. It can so narrow our trust and expectations of other human beings that we cannot even enter into promises by which to build a new future. Worship as memory without hope is thus not a rehearsal of faith at all but of nostalgia, resentment, or vengefulness.

This rehearsal of our ultimate relationships is not merely an exercise of will to struggle toward that end. As rehearsal, worship also affirms the ways these patterns are already realized in our midst, enabling us to participate in them symbolically through rituals, songs, poems, and movements. The words, symbols, and rituals of worship already create a world into which we seek to act, a drama we already begin to enact. In the symbolic life of worship we act out the way the ultimate purposes of God are "already but not yet." It is a dress rehearsal for the interplay of life we also anticipate in often unnoticed acts of love, beauty, and justice.

CRITICAL CULTURAL ENGAGEMENT

This dialogue between the archaic and the future is echoed in the critical dialectic between church and culture that must also exist in our worship. Our symbols and rituals must both incorporate and critically transform the relationships we trust in our everyday life. In the monarchical era the trust people put in kings and queens permeated the symbolism of worship. Simultaneously, this model of rule was reshaped by the image of Christ's kingship as one of service, self-sacrifice, and obedience to God's law in nature and in scripture. The symbols of our everyday trust in democracy, republican governance, federal order, constitutions, and conciliar decision-making ought to inform our worship but also be transformed by enduring theological values. That is to say, our worship symbols should have a certain "assonance" with those of the surrounding culture. They resonate in some ways but clash dissonantly in others.

The symbol of Pentecost, for instance, both resonates with the international assemblies necessary for global governance and, with its underlying image of a unifying spirit, goes beyond them. An effort at symbolic assonance arises in many American churches, where an American flag is juxtaposed to a "Christian" flag in the sanctuary. The question here is which flag "wins"? Which symbol shapes the other? Is this true assonance, even dissonance, or is it mere reduction of Christian faith to American patriotism? Such questions open up the whole matter of how our symbolism of God's republic is related concretely to the various civil religions of our world.

Similarly, in light of Christ's type of presidency we can see how the ordinary presidents around us ought to preside through the power of persuasive vision rather than through the cynical manipulation of special interests and the fears of isolated individuals. Constitutions need to be transparent to the deeper covenants of people and the land in the face of the Author of Creation's drama. They also must be open to God's more expansive covenant with all of creation. The law by which we live has to be more than a torturous wall of fear and mistrust; it must be transformed in light of ongoing public conversation. It must reflect, however dimly, the symbolic anticipation of a republic in which the spirit of a God presides who purposes for us the shalom of a new creation. Clearly, all of these ideals reveal tremendous gaps between our own practices and the purposes of God.

In this way our worship is not merely a rehearsal of a future goal but also the enactment of a moral conversation between who we are and what we might become. It takes seriously our partial moral achievements even as it exposes them to the awesome possibilities that still lie ahead. It takes up our present natures to entertain a grace that both condemns our arrogance and nourishes our hope. It reflects God's work in creation as well as in a world to come. The Passion Week before Easter is one example of this dialectic, in which one model of perfected governance is celebrated on Palm Sunday, only to be put through the fire of reversal, betrayal, and death. The resurrection story from Easter to Pentecost then begins to reconstruct a different model of governance, which overthrows our assumptions of liberation and rule while opening our eyes to wider possibilities of communication, the sharing of gifts, and mutual care.

Critical cultural engagement must also take account of the way symbols function in specific cultures and societies. The symbol of kingship functioned in medieval European society both to reinforce and to humble the claims of kings. The symbol also could set forth the ways actual kings fell short of their proper care for their subjects—all, of course, within a paternalistic framework. Similarly, the symbol of republic or democracy can have ambivalent meanings for people. In South Africa the descendants of Dutch settlers, the Boers, fled from British imperial rule to establish republics (but not on a fully democratic basis), which then reinforced the subjugation of the native African peoples. For the subjugated peoples, the laws of the British Empire, which tried to overcome racial discrimination in the law, then looked relatively benign in comparison. Similarly, the American republic known as the United States also produced bitter fruit for the original inhabitants of North America as well as for the enslaved Africans brought to its shores. The point here is that no symbol can guarantee actual justice. These symbols are the language and grammar in which we seek to work out our understandings of God's justice and work among us. The point of the major shift in political symbolism I am considering is not to find words that will save us from our sin but to worship in the language of our actual ethical aspirations. To speak another language is, I believe, to engage in a kind of symbolic self-deception.

PSYCHOLOGICAL DEPTH

Our fifth principle claims that worship must have psychological as well as political depth. Not only must worship link our past and future, our present culture and our eschatological cult, it must also link our innermost emotional life with the widest relationships of God's creation. Without these connections worship cannot tend to the motivational task as well as to the presentational task I focused on earlier. This is an awesome challenge. What does this claim mean?

One of the critical achievements of monarchical worship was that it enabled people to take the model of trustworthy relationship they ideally experienced with their mothers and fathers and translate it to wider systems of governance. The king or queen was a parent to the people, whose kin he or she was, at least fictively. Deep emotional bonds of dependence, trust, and fierce loyalty were transferred to local lord, distant king or queen, and a lofty hidden emperor. Liturgy could then ride this line of connection between parent and monarch with a recitation of our adoption as God's heavenly children. In the phrases of the American Social Gospel tradition, it could rehearse "the Fatherhood of God and the brotherhood of man."[2]

Even people's basic understanding of the natural order could be patterned after this parental relationship. In theories of the "great chain of being" going back to classical times, the natural order could be seen as a descent of grades of being from the fullness of the parent— almost like the mother's womb—to the bare existence of lesser orders below. Likewise, with the rise of evolution, the development of all of life could be construed in terms of the development from infant to adult. Primitive cultures were somehow more infantile and childlike; citified cultures mature and adult. Sigmund Freud and the psychoanalytic schools could then turn this around to see ways in which our whole evolutionary inheritance was replicated in the maturation of each self. In short, with one model we could navigate worlds of governance and physics, reinforcing a sense of trust and security about our place in the universe.

The rise of republican models of governance challenges us to rethink these dimensions of our life. Unless we can find new ways of relating our psychological and familial life to this model of governance we can neither trust it nor commit ourselves in worship to visions of its redemption. I have already pointed out how the church has preserved a monarchical paradigm of governance in its worship by translating it into a psychological model of self-control over our passions. This way of construing the relationship of monarchical worship to our public life has now been undermined by the rise of the egalitarian norm for marriage. The psychological monarchy of the male self was reinforced by the little monarchy of the family and rehearsed in worship. At the same time, however, this psychologization of worship already began to individualize each believer as a little self-determining kingdom. A sense of full and equal citizenship for each believer, male and female, has gradually pressed couples to engage in the kind of communication, mutual respect, negotiation, and promise-making hitherto reserved for a democratic public. The democratization of the family, with its implications for child development, further marginalizes the monarchical paradigm for our psychological lives as well as for worship.

The democratization of family life was already under way with the seventeenth-century Puritans' conception of the family as a little commonwealth in which people were to be trained up into covenant with God and with their fellow citizens. While this ideal was countered by the resurgence of paternal and monarchical ideals in the nineteenth-century conception of the family as a Gothic retreat, it has found expression today in the extension of many civil rights to children, promotion of conciliar approaches to family decisions, and the use of contractual thinking in negotiating rules and activities with them. Through an increased attention to parental relationships of respect, mutuality, communication, and negotiation, parents seek to inculcate the values of democratic citizenship in their children.

The patterns of communication and negotiation experienced by couples and families echo and reinforce the conventions of civility necessary to public life. But children are still children, not adults. There really are differences between parents and children that demand our recognition. Children's need for care, nurture, dependence, trust, control, and benevolent instruction is still high. Paternalism and maternalism still have their own ethical validity. The point is not to eliminate parental relations and their symbolic presence in worship, but to relate them to the fuller public life to which we are called. The Puritan model provides some helpful insights. We need to expand on it with perspectives drawn from fields as diverse as developmental psychology, contemporary physics, and management theory, not to mention other cultural models of the relation of family to public councils. Because this is such a vast and difficult set of topics, I can only indicate some possibly fruitful explorations into the basis for knitting together our psychological life with our public life.

Our basic starting point is to affirm the way we are active constructors of meaning from the beginning. Our lived experience is "agential," meaning we seek to be agents in the construction of our world. We seek a fullness of action. Even as our parents and other adults seek to take care of us according to their understandings, values, and purposes, we transform their action upon us, coloring it with meanings, even twisting it to our purposes. Sometimes we construct a world of meaning that is actually a closet of confusion and perversity. We are unable to establish a shared world with others, a little public in which we can continue to expand our repertoire, try on new roles for ourselves, and find a wider confirmation of our hunches about reality. The point of parenting, as well as one of the points of worship, is to help us negotiate and navigate this passage from infantile privation to adult participation. It does so in part by rehearsing the manifold ways in which we are drawn into communication, giving voice to our inner imaginations. The challenges of public worship can lead us to listen to the possible voices emerging from strange experience beyond us and help us enter into ever-expanding covenants of trust with others and with the natural world. Worship can grant us all, children and adults, a certain equality as we struggle with our fears of shame, our lack of courage, our perplexity and trembling in the face of the unknown, and our mistrust of a humanity that has shown itself to be more cruel than any creature of the night. In worship we can create a shared world that both enfolds our anxiety and cultivates our hope in the face of the wider republic into which God calls us.

Not only are we agential beings seeking a wider publicity and confirmation, we are also covenantal beings. The confirmation we seek in our acts demands that we enter into promissory bonds with others. This is the biblical meaning of love as covenantal faithfulness, a kind of public love that establishes a world of common meaning and trust. Our acting is to be oriented toward our covenantal bonds with others. Covenant and publicity are the legs with which we walk into the symbolic world of worship and the daily world of human interaction. Here we find a psychology focused not on the self-control or even self-knowledge typical of a monarchical psychology, but one shaped by our nature as covenantal actors. Surely much more needs to be done here to develop such a psychology further. My only purpose is to lay out a principle that must be attended to if worship is to do its work and be a genuine rehearsal of God's great public.

Sensory Holism

The sixth principle that must inform our regeneration of worship is aesthetic. Worship must employ all our senses if we are to enter into communication with the divine mystery of salvation. Protestant Christians, especially those in the Calvinist tradition, have focused almost exclusively on words within a theology of the Word. While this has done much to foster the kind of conciliar speech indispensable to public life, it has also robbed us of the symbolic resources not only to communicate more fully but to dramatize the underlying patterns of divine right order that can legitimate and critique our public life. Such dramatic symbolism is much more than verbal. It involves vision, motion, smell, touch, and taste. Only through the whole panoply of the senses can we recover the "commune" in communicate.

Put differently, such symbolic communication recovers our whole bodies as instruments and receptors. This is not just a matter of Protestant "ear people" recovering the visual arts. It is also a matter of Catholic "eye people" entering more deeply into a discourse beyond imitation of models, obedience to commands, and rote responses to fixed rituals. For both it is a matter of moving beyond the isolation of reading, praying, or adoring alone to a full bodily participation in a complex ensemble of public interchange. It is a matter of taking seriously the resurrection of the body as a present reality in the assembly of the faithful. This new body is not merely a matter of the age to come but is indispensable to an affirmation of publicity within the present creation. Bodily presence is the way we are public, distinguishable, unique beings. It is the way we communicate with each other as a part of this creation. Public interaction, interdependence, dialogue, and mutual care are only possible within this finitude of bodily existence, and it is this existence that is to be redeemed from death and the anxiety that cripples our love.[3]

For many Christians, especially Protestants, the longing for a richer aesthetic of worship and communication leads them back to the symbolic richness of a preverbal era. The dazzling splendors of medieval cathedrals, the haunting simplicity of Gregorian chant, and the icons of Orthodoxy liberate them from an often suffocating absorption in didactic literalism and legalism. What is problematic in this recovery of the senses is the panoply of monarchical governance paradigms celebrated so powerfully in these artistic forms. This is, after all, the art of a patriarchal monarchical world. Feminist critics have done much to reduce the overwhelming presence of patriarchal governance symbols by pressing back to pre-Christian art and to works by and about women from the Christian era. What is needed now is both a recovery of the aesthetics of the conciliar strands in Christianity and a cultivation of new artistic environments. We need to generate a new aesthetics congruent with the political paradigms we seek to rehearse in worship. We need to press to an aesthetics beyond Christendom.

How is this to be done? We can only touch on a few points here. Such an artistic move in architecture involves supplanting the nave with the circle. In music, folk idioms, antiphons, and a variety of musical instruments need to balance our five-hundred-year fixation on the mighty organ. In the visual arts, abstraction as well as representational art in many media can open up new vistas and sensibilities for us, especially to overcome the racial, religious, and cultural ghettos in which most of us live. All of this is quite beyond the scope of this book or my capabilities, but it must be lifted up as a crucial principle in the regeneration of worship.

A Consistent Grammar

Finally, worship must develop within its entire movement a consistent "grammar." The entire action of worship should enact a dramatic trajectory. It should unfold a chain of events in which each link is important and serves a function. Only in this way can we rehearse a paradigm of right order that touches the many dimensions of our lives and yet weaves them into a whole. Much of Protestant worship is simply a collection of traditional acts without any sense of the whole. Each Sunday different hymns, prayers, anthems, and sermon themes are plugged into the slots in the program, with no attention given to the overall structure. We are left with a series of experiences that appeal to our feelings but no great story in which we can rehearse the ultimate meaning of our lives.

This lack of attention to a consistent grammar appears strikingly in our practice of changing individual words or phrases within a hymn or prayer. Efforts at inclusivity change or neutralize the gender of individual words but not the overall political paradigm within which the hymn is moving. The search for a general paradigm presses us beyond such tinkering to a reconstruction of the underlying patterns themselves. It presses us beyond vocabulary to grammar.

For some people such an appeal to a consistent grammar sounds not only constrictive but idolatrous. For them the patchwork and bric-a-brac of much worship provide holes through which God's transcendent holiness can shine. But this, it seems to me, is a one-sided notion of transcendence—the God of gaps and holes—that relies almost solely on the classic Protestant concern with idolatry rather than the typical Catholic concern with incarnate presence. Protestants have historically made the First and Second Commandments' prohibitions of "other gods" and "graven images" central to their theology. Extended into worship it meant the destruction of visual arts in the churches. Calvin's austere auditorium in Geneva would become the model for Protestant worship. Only scripture, prayer, and preaching would remain. Catholics have always upheld the role of visual and other arts as media for worship. The idea of sacrament appeals to all the artistic means embedded in the creation, which, it is assumed, can become, like Mary's womb and Christ's body, a bearer of divine grace.[4]

The program I am urging here asks first for some "Catholic substance" for our images of our ultimate relationship with God and each other. The articulation of transcendence urged by Protestant tradition then occurs not only in the gap between our symbols and God's reality but in the awesome divide between our actual lives and the aspirations we seek to live into in worship. Our sense of transcendence is then tied to the mysterious freedom and fidelity with which God seeks to draw us into this ultimately trustworthy relationship. The political paradigms of our worship can then point us to that trustworthy public this mysterious and yet faithful God is drawing us to. Our effort for a consistent grammar of worship springs from a desire to bring our worship into congruence with the cosmic character of this divine activity.

These seven principles at least give us some orientation to the task before us. Surely others are necessary for such a project, though seven is a time-honored number. Through pursuit of these principles we can seek to honor both the theological and ethical integrity of our task as well as the deep-seated dynamics of worship in various cultural contexts. The struggle for worship forms that honor our political ethics as well as the traditions and sensibilities of our worship cultures is difficult. The purpose of this book is to identify that challenge, orient us to a response, and, in this last part, to explore some possible practices that might better enable us to pray for the coming of God's republic.

Praying for God's Republic: A Worship Fantasy

I BEGAN THESE REFLECTIONS by arguing that we ought to move from monarchical to republican paradigms in our worship life. Symbols, language, and rituals drawing on our longing for trustworthy publicity within God's comprehensive covenant need to shape our worship life of prayer, song, and testimony. Such a move is rooted in ancient theological claims, our own need for ethical integrity, and the apologetic demands of witness in a world of democracies and republics yearning for their birth, renewal, or transformation.

In the previous chapter I set forth some possible principles to guide us in the audacious task of transforming our worship in this direction. First, our worship has to present us with patterns of our ultimate trustworthy relationships. Worship should provide us with a drama through which we can participate symbolically in the hopes, failures, and renewals of our moral and spiritual life together. At the same time our worship has to be motivationally effective, so it can draw on our deep longings even as it transforms these motivations. It must be able to take the heated commitments fired by our nostalgia and self-interest and turn them to wider longings for expansive publics and a new creation. The work of presentation and of motivation occurs in the active rehearsal of our relation with God, a rehearsal that we call worship.

In line with these overarching principles I went on to say that such worship should take the primary form of a participatory assembly in which we rehearse God's covenant with creation and renew our commitment to it. This creates the "constitution" of our assembly as Christians. This covenantal renewal needs to look forward to the mysterious perfection of God's purposes. This focus on God's *eschaton*—God's end—gives us a transcendent point from which to be critically engaged with the culture around us. Even as we appropriate the language and symbols of democratic republican life we must transform them in a critical manner rooted in our most powerful theological convictions.

Such an appropriation of political symbolism must also grasp deep psychological motivations and link them to the widest arenas of public life and cosmic evolution. To do this, worship has to occur in ways that reach all our senses. Finally, such a sensory holism has to occur within a worship that speaks a consistent grammar. Our theological intentions press us to a worship that expresses a coherent drama of God's creative and redemptive work and our participation in it.

The question at this point is: What worship practices ought to emerge within such a perspective? Changes in worship are difficult and occur over long periods of time. Moreover, we usually think that such changes should be made in ways that hide our human intentions so that the changes look "natural" or even of divine origin. Worship buried in the mists of the past thus tends to have more authority than the rites, songs, and prayers springing forth out of whole cloth from a committee. Nevertheless, all significant worship changes occur because of human decisions. Sometimes these decisions are to formalize somewhat spontaneous developments—such as the passing of the peace—and sometimes it is clearly a carefully thought out plan—as with any hymnal or prayer book. Both, however, demand our personal initiative. Changes in worship occur as a kind of "radical gradualism"—a curious phrase that captures the necessary tensions in such an enterprise. These reflections are part of such a process.

How then might we worship in the light of God's republic? At this point I would like to walk through a fantasy of how such a rehearsal of our faith might go. Such a walk will consist of selected perceptions gathered from my own experience in worship and efforts at innovation by others. In this imagined worship, questions of cultural context, particular heritage, and to a certain extent socioeconomic class, while important, are not in the foreground of concern. The point here is to lift up the distinctive contributions of a worship symbolism shaped by covenantal-federal and democratic-republican symbols of governance.

A WORSHIP FANTASY

We approach a simple building whose entrance features a small court-yard with running water and a few ornamental trees. The building's foundation is square but supports a circular hall under a dome that admits reflected light into the interior. As we enter the main assembly we can see that it could seat around four hundred people in sturdy folding chairs circled around the room. Looking to my left I see that the pool outside seems to have followed us into the room, forming a baptismal pool with some additional plants fed by the filtered light. Four aisles emerging from doors that seem to be on the axes of the compass flow toward the center, where a natural wood round table almost five feet in diameter sits on a low dais. On the table is an artistic arrangement of Japanese iris around a wooden cross encircled with barbed wire. Four plates of whole wheat bread and four chalices are placed at the table's "compass points." A brightly colored cloth lies folded next to each plate.

Looking around, we see no organ, just speakers. Two microphones are placed on stands at opposite points next to the table. A transparent lectern stands beside each microphone. There are no national or "Christian" flags but rather brightly colored banners and cloths on the walls. A combo occupies a section to one side; they play quietly while people hum along.

Presently a woman enters with a deliberate pace and walks to the table. A man (I later find out he is the president of the church council) picks up a mike in a formal fashion and gives it to her. She then says to us: "Come, gathering Spirit, constitute our assembly with your power, your justice, and your peace. Bring in all who labor and are heavily burdened, bring in the proud and the despairing, form us into your people, eager for your new creation. Let us begin again."

At this point everyone rises, the combo strikes up jauntily, and a procession of children comes in from one of the doors carrying papers, drawings, and cutouts (are they of animals?) that they place on the round table. With them are, I presume, their teachers, but then even more adults keep coming in. I realize that this is the procession of people who have been studying in various classes for the last hour. I later find out that they, including the children, have all been working on biblical texts or stories relating to the same theme—reconciliation. I realize I have already missed half the program!

We start singing a simple, lilting song, almost a waltz, with words asking that God give us the light, power, and peace of God's new republic.

At the conclusion, the woman presiding says: "Listen, everyone! We convene this assembly in the name of Jesus, who has promised to preside among us always."

The people respond: "We claim our citizenship in this place."

Then another person gets up and is given a microphone. He lifts up his hands, saying: "Come Creator Spirit, mystery of the galaxies, power of supernovae, magnetism of love. Attune our ears, open our eyes, infuse our hearts, so that we can hear, and speak, and have courage to follow the One who died for our sakes."

Again, the people respond: "Preside among us today, O Christ."

The two speakers replace their microphones and sit down. Two others get up, take two cloths from the table, and walk over to a young man sitting nervously in the front row. He is dressed simply in a white cotton cloth suit like men wear in India in the hottest months. One of the two takes him by the hand and leads him back to the pool, where two other people are standing to greet and hug him. They introduce him as David, and talk about his desire to enter into full participation in the assembly's life. David says a few words about the wanderings and searchings of his own life, how he hid so much of his life from others and lived in fear. He then talks of his desire to take on the spirit he has found in the people here and in the life of Jesus and some of Jesus' followers he has read about.

One escort walks into the pool with him while the other, a woman, says: "We have glimpsed, we have tasted, we have listened with aching ears to an emerging public of God's presence, where we can speak and listen in trust, where we can confess our innermost thoughts and be received. We have been touched by the beauty of God in creation and by the conversation of our songs. Here we claim the beginnings of a new world, the republic of God's peace. In this spirit we now recognize David's entrance into the inauguration of this new creation and participation in God's republic of peace."

She asks David: "Do you covenant today with this assembly and with the God who upholds it to seek its justice, participate in its pain and joy, and receive its forgiveness when you fail?" He answers: "I covenant this with all my life." She then says: "We therefore wash you free of your past, lead you into the waters of rebirth, and baptize you in the spirit of the One who has founded, liberated, and empowers this creation beyond all time and space."

The assembly then says: "We confirm your citizenship among us and covenant to stand with you according to the constitution of Christ and the faithfulness of God."

As he stands in the pool, they take two large shells and pour water all over him. When the people hear the pouring of the water they break into applause. As his sponsors dry him with their cloths and then lead him out of the pool through a side door the people start singing a song expressing thanks for this renewal of life—not only his but all of theirs as well.

Another person then gets up, is given the microphone in the usual manner, and lifts up a prayer of gratitude for life's continuation and renewal in spite of human greed and destructiveness. She concludes with a prayer that God still preside in our midst in patient and persistent persuasiveness.

The people then join in a kind of litany, with the presider saying: "Even as you have called us, O God, so now we call on you to hear the prayers and petitions of our hearts: For us, who are often weary, frenzied, and driven by anxiety and fear."

Then the people respond: "Renew your spirit among your people, O God."

"For neighbors broken in divorce and death, in bankruptcy and unemployment."

The people respond: "Renew your spirit among your people, O God."

"For the drug addicted, the AIDS afflicted, the hungry, homeless, and assaulted."

The people again: "Renew your spirit among your people, O God."
"Among the powerful work out your purposes. Among the violent
work your patient power of persuasion."

The people say: "Renew your spirit among your people, O God."

There follows a brief time during which individuals pray for friends,
situations, and causes, with various responses from the group. A young
child takes a microphone to anyone who requests it. The person presiding then says: "We lay all these concerns and petitions on your table,
O God. We publish them in this assembly, offering them in a spirit of
brokenness and yet of hope for your patient power of peace. Reconcile
your world, reconstitute the assemblies of your people, and lead us
into your new creation."

Everyone breaks into a simple song with the refrain "May it be so
and soon."

At that point the woman who began the worship is given a mike.
She says: "Let's talk about the spirit of reconciliation that constitutes
the core of our life together." What follows, with some passing around
of mikes and some use of the lectern, is a kind of conversation, much
of which is based on Bible texts they had studied earlier. The children
rehearse a little skit based on Matthew's passage about handling dis-
putes in the church. It is clear that the speakers have been schooled in a
certain style of presentation that is personal, short, and to the point.
The way they hold together heartfelt emotion (one man even starts
weeping) with public restraint is impressive. (I find out later that all
new members are involved in an educational program to help them
participate in the worship.) The presider moves the conversation along
and at a certain point wraps up a couple of key ideas, moves to the
table, and says:

> O God, our Creator, for our lives we give you thanks.
> O God, our Redeemer, for our salvation we give you thanks.
> O God, our Wisdom, for the light of your truth we give you thanks.
> When we were warring tribes you gave us the covenant of your law.
> When we were locked in legalities you gave us your grace.

When we made of our faith a fortress you broke down the walls with the power of your freedom.

When we asked for a king to conquer our enemies you gave us a teacher whose spirit presides among us today.

When we hid in the darkness of our anxiety and fear you led us out into the light of your assembly.

In creation, in exodus, in Jesus, and in all your saints you have been marvelously faithful to us.

Now, in this meal of memory and hope help us to renew our faithfulness to you and your covenantal purposes.

Four people along the outside then stand up and walk down the four aisles carrying identical large placards; they hold them up facing the people in their section. The one presiding says: "Let us remember and renew our covenant with God, with each other, and with the whole creation." The response goes something like this:

"With gratitude to God for this sustaining creation, we covenant to be transmitters of the gracious life we have received. With gratitude for God's emancipating faithfulness, we covenant to struggle against our self-absorption and despair. With gratitude for God's inauguration of a new republic of trust, truth, and beauty, we covenant to care for all creation—our food, our shelter, and the great theater of God's promises and mercy all our days."

The people then begin singing a soft song asking for God's Spirit and Wisdom as they come to a table open to strangers as well as friends. They ask Christ to preside at this table in power and peace. By this time the newly baptized person and sponsors are seated in the first row. They present the newly baptized with a special cloth as a sign of his membership and say: "David, receive this cloth of bright colors as a sign of your service at Christ's table and your participation in his presidency among this assembly. May the inauguration of your new life this day publish God's reconciling spirit in every aspect of your life."

David then gets up and begins a prayer that the people have evidently memorized.

O Founding Spirit,
Only you are holy,
Govern us with perfect justice,
Give us all the food we need,
Forgive our sin as we forgive our enemies.
Save us from the judgment day and
Deliver us from evil powers.
May your great republic come. Amen.

At this point, a girl and a boy come from opposite sides of the hall carrying menorah-like candelabras. All eyes follow the flickering flames in silence as the candelabras are placed on opposite sides of the table. The boy and girl then say together: "The people's table is ready. Our president is here."

The people then say: "We come to the table, we respond to your call."

Two of the presiders then get up, pick up cloths, place them on their forearms, and say: "The whole creation is called to a table of nurture and conversation. Hewn from the forests, finished with care, the table is round, for all persons are equal. The table is full, because God is gracious and bountiful. The table is marked with the candles and the cross of the one whose spirit presides here forever—a spirit of exodus, of renewal, and of promise. It is also circled with barbed wire to remind us of the suffering of fellow citizens of the globe who are held in the darkness of fear. While we long for the fullness of their presence, we also are bold to taste from the presidential banquet yet to come. Come, now, the table is ready if you are ready to receive its spirit."

The people respond: "Come, Spirit of Life, preside in our midst."

The combo then quietly backs up a simple song—"I'm Gonna Sit at the Welcome Table." People proceed to the table, bringing offerings they place in plates held at each aisle. When they take the bread, the servers say: "Take of God's body and renew the earth." When they take the cup, they say: "May Christ preside among us through his sacrifice." People respond with various words of acceptance.

At the end of the round table ritual, the offering plates are placed on the table and one of the servers speaks a prayer of dedication, praying that these offerings of our private resources will serve the wider public of God's purposes.

At that point two women (Kathy and Margaret) and a couple (Stan and Patricia) come forward to the table. One of the presiders stands up, first addressing the two women. She explains to the assembly that the women are going away for a yearlong service project with a group of churches in Guatemala. She says to them: "Kathy and Margaret, we commission you in the spirit of this table and this assembly to work and live with peaceful purpose and unflagging hope. Help us as well as those you will be with to sense more deeply the trust and power of the Great Republic to which the whole creation is called."

She then explains that Stan and Patricia have agreed to lead a task force on low-income housing in the community. To them, she says: "Stan and Patricia, in the spirit of this table of hospitality and hope we commission you to help people unlock God's bounty, so that everyone will have decent and affordable housing in our community. May you preside with patience, encouragement, and purpose, mobilizing the despairing and reconciling the contentious, so that all might taste the power of God's peace."

After shaking hands all around, both couples light a candle from the candelabras and walk down the aisle. The presider then lifts her arms up and prays:

O God of our hopes, help us live by your hope.
O God of love, help us live by your love.
O God of justice, help us live by your truth.
Even as you have elected us to be your people, may we continually elect you to preside among us,
> that justice might abound where evil has prevailed,
> that reason might shine where fear has made us blind,
> that the spirit of service would melt the bondage of pride
> and the little circle of our friends become the Great Republic of your peace.
May it be so and may it be soon. Amen.

With that, the combo strikes up a rousing song affirming their citizenship in God's republic and asking for courage in their baptismal calling to exercise that citizenship in the face of the world's indifference and hostility. At its conclusion, a presider asks us to link our hands and says: "And now, let us go into the world in peace, knowing that our constitution is God's peace, our new creation is God's promise, and God's spirit presides among us to the end of time. Amen." With an upbeat arrangement from the combo the assembly dissolves into conversation and exchange, the children retrieve their offerings from the table, and people begin slow exits to their ordinary life and time.

REFLECTING ON THE WORSHIP

This account is part experience and part fantasy. We can take it as an image of one way people might rehearse the coming of God's republic in a renewed creation. No words can convey the rich images, associations, and sensations of an actual experience, but this report can help us reflect on some of the elements of such a worship.

Some of these elements are rather obvious in their meaning and importance for this political reconstruction of our worship. That the building accommodates only about four hundred people is dictated by the requirements of a participatory public. It must be larger than a friendship circle but small enough to enable people to speak and to listen to one another. Worship is neither a social gathering nor a spectator sport. The church is neither living room nor stadium; it is rooted in the life of a participatory public. The circular shape of the building and of the worship setting has an immediate affinity with democratic themes of equality, participation, and mutual recognition.[1] At the same time, the circle is a cross laid out on the points of the compass to remind participants of their relation to a globe that stretches in every direction. In reaching out to the globe it makes a statement about the interpenetration of global structure and human politics. This is quite different from the classic elongated cross with its head pointed toward the east or toward Jerusalem. Such an architecture was tied directly to the sacrificial crucifixion and the dominance of history over nature.

The circled cross represents an effort to focus more on the democratic assembly of the spirit in a creation longing for global renewal. The theme of bondage and sacrifice, as symbolized by the barbed wire, is related to the struggle for liberation into a public that gathers round a table for council and nurture.

The round table has become an important symbol of democratic conversation, not to mention the way it brings together the experience of communion and council—pivotal experiences in the life of the Christian assembly. The way water, light, and even vegetation carries from exterior to interior speaks of our connection with the whole of creation, especially through baptism—what Don Saliers calls the "water bath"—and the table. At several points the compass of longitude and latitude reminds participants that they are part of a wider world.

Democratic themes also infuse the way the microphone, a weighty symbol of authority in a world struggling for publicity, is given by the representative of the assembly to the presider of the moment. It is also passed around and made available to every participant. The cloth, which also functions as a towel, displaces or reconstructs the stole. It is a mark of service and is picked up and laid down in order to designate certain presiding functions. In all these respects the assembly rehearses the way leadership in the assembly is a matter of function rather than permanent status. It is the servant Messiah who is always presiding through those who pick up the towel and the microphone. This motif of service is echoed politically in the dynamic of election. The Christ is a public servant, not primarily in the sense of meeting our immediate felt needs or interests but as one who builds and sustains the public in which we find expression and confirmation for our lives. Thus, our usual symbols of presidency are reshaped by notions of presidership and assembly-building.

At a somewhat less pronounced but still obvious level, the assembly establishes its connection with the historic people of Israel. The presence of a menorah, at least in basic design, signifies the primary context in which Jesus is seen as the Christ—the anointed one, the elected one. The menorah, like Passover, recalls themes of emancipation and renewal. Its necessary presence illuminates what the gathering of the table is about, and from it the newest people elected to extend the public's power take their light—an image of the way Christianity is only an extension of the faith born within Israel's womb. Certainly, these critical motifs do not solve all the issues standing between Christians and Jews—only concrete historical action can do that—but they remind the assembly of its ongoing connection with their elder descendants of the Book of books.

Some things are important by virtue of their absence. There is no organ here, which would disappoint many who love its sonority, range, and literature. This choice is probably one of ethos more than stewardship and finances; that is, the organ functions preeminently to organize and dominate a large crowd. It is associated not only with a large budget but great training. The combo, while it can require much skill, bears with it a greater closeness to the people—not only their budget but their music and abilities. For a gathering of three or four hundred, it assists the people's singing without dominating it. The people hear each other rather than the musicians leading them.

While much of this worship will be familiar in form and substance to many Christians, it may also be jarring because of the absence of the reading of scripture. This is a perplexing problem in that the mythic paradigms of scripture are dominated, though not exclusively so, by monarchical themes. We have already experienced various attempts to rephrase the texts in gender-inclusive ways. Some of these are happy efforts, others are not. Even worse, from a political perspective, was the ancient substitution of "Lord" for the reading of the mystical name for the Holy One of Israel—Yahweh. Here, in order to avoid giving the Holy One a proper name, readers reduced Yahweh to a particular governance symbol of lordship. Rather than denigrate God, they ended up absolutizing lords. Thus, rephrasing the scriptural words to fit theological demands is not a new practice. The demands to change the dominant paradigm of worship only pose new challenges for this practice.

The practice the congregation above engages in is to make the reading of scripture part of its educational program, so that the Scriptures are not simply ritualized as a symbol but studied as a record. People can compare translations, reflect on their meaning, their language, and their relationship to our present life and future prospects. This study then sets up the themes that are carried through ritually in the worship activity proper. Theologically, then, the "educational" program is not an optional and additional activity but an integral prerequisite for worship. The worship itself can then rehearse the stories or themes without being bound by the very language and paradigms in which they emerge. Such a move is historically both Catholic and Protestant. It is Catholic in that it sees worship clearly as a ritual symbolic activity that needs to engage the governance of our lives in a holistic and coherent manner. It is Protestant in that scripture is seen as important, but also as something that needs to be studied, interpreted, and explicated. In order to do this, many Protestant churches turned worship into an extended exposition of scripture. The assembly for worship became a school of the Bible. The congregation above is trying for a balance that gives priority to worship as rehearsal of our right governance before God.

Similarly, creedal components and what is traditionally called the Lord's Prayer appear in a transmuted form, drawing on their ancient forms as models and archetypes but not as rote formulas. Here again the worship seeks to capture original intent within a coherent vision of what worship is rehearsing. The covenant reaffirmed by the assembly as well as some of the prayers also follow a trinitarian form without a slavish obedience to their particular symbolizations.

Connected to the problem of reading of scripture is that of the choice of words referring to God. I have already commented on the way the name of the inexpressible mystery at the heart of the universe has been reduced, ironically, to one of the pettier roles in the symbolism of feudal kingship. Many people, such as Brian Wren, Sallie McFague, Ruth Duck, and others, have struggled to expand our repertoire of symbols in order to avoid pinning one image on such a holy mystery. This has been an important move, although people show a remarkable lack of imagination in this regard in ordinary worship. What has been neglected, however, is what this move against idolatry does to our rehearsal of any coherent sense of ultimate governing relationships. This visionary dimension needs attention now, not to attenuate the plurality of our words but to take account of the role they play in articulating a coherent faithfulness about our relationship with God, with one another, and with creation. This sense of faithful relationship originally lay at the heart of what the Latin West called "religion." This claiming of "true religion" (one of Calvin's favorite phrases) is being worked out in our articulation of a covenantal and republican vision of governance.

In placing symbols of covenant, public, and democracy at the center of our vision, we evoke terms like *president, promise, public, people, assembly,* and *covenant.* In this assembly's worship God is not directly called "president," in part because to do so might reinforce a monarchical image of presidency rather than imply in God the peculiar dynamics of a presidency shaped by Jesus' mission and ministry. It is much more the Holy Spirit who is said to preside—the active form of the word—in the assembly. The action of presiding—with its aspects of mobilizing, encouraging, visioning, ordering, moderating, and bringing to consensus—is more important than the position or status of president. Moreover, through the symbolism of the towel, presiding is rehearsed as a table service to the assembly so that it might come closer to being a perfect public of trust circled around a table of God's bounty.

The work of presidency is no more evident than in the way the "sermon" occurs. It is not the proclamation of one voice lifted above the others by training, ordination, or employment. Rather, it is a process of speaking and listening in which the presider seeks to draw people out and together to the extent possible in light of their hearing of that day's theme. The "Word" can still be understood in terms of the Greek *logos,* but logos has here the meaning of being a pattern of discourse and conversation rather than a simple command from a monarch who stands outside the people's election and citizenship.

This kind of God who presides in the spirit of service to a saving public is not praised like a narcissistic king. Gratitude is indeed critical to the way the assembly stated its covenant and acknowledged the gifts they had received, but it does not become the basis for the kind of kowtowing associated with ancient and modern despots alike.

The citizenship model that underlies the conception of the self in worship is articulated in several ways, but most evidently in baptism. The baptism occurred near the beginning of the fantasy worship service so that the one being baptized and the whole assembly could join together in affirming the sense of inauguration, of entry into citizenship, of emergence out of their private into their common public world. The person being baptized made a genuine profession of faith as a crossing over—a passing over—from the privations of despair, anxiety, or self-absorption into the saving public in which he was heard, confirmed, and given voice. The waters of baptism, of course, resonate with many other associations. I am only highlighting the way the baptismal ritual begins life in a new public constituted by God's wisdom and governed by Christ's presidency.

If I were to talk further with members of that assembly, they might have told me that they do indeed have a kind of baptism for infants, but that that action occurs at the time of commissioning at the end, when people dedicate themselves to particular paths and projects in the spirit of the assembly. Here, the critical and demanding task of parenthood is lifted up and the parents and the people covenant to nurture the child in the spirit of the assembly so that one day he or she can claim his or her citizenship in a fuller way.

Obviously, we could reflect on many other motifs even in this short account. The point here is to begin the conversation about specific ways we might speak a different language and sing in a new key about the ultimate relationships governing our lives in this creation and "beyond." The weekly particularities of ordinary worship are where we must begin if we are to rehearse the relationships we believe sustain us. However, we need not stop there. One further aspect worth considering is the way we rehearse the seasons by which we cycle through the terrestrial year.

RE-CENTERING THE LITURGICAL YEAR

Even though biblical faith is historical and "linear," Christians and Jews have always used the solar or lunar year to rehearse the key dramas of their faith. The cycle of nature has provided the scaffold for our ascent into an open future. Moreover, the construction of this liturgical year has helped us keep the historical and natural dimensions of our faith lives together. The question is not how to escape these seasonal constructions but what constructions to employ. What kind of liturgical cycle best honors our commitment to the renewal of creation and our pilgrimage to an unimaginable new republic of freedom and power?

Our first step is to take a global perspective and realize that the Northern and Southern hemispheres experience the natural cycle differently. Even within hemispheres there can be vast differences in the relation of people to natural cycles of growth, harvest, and dormancy. A search for a global faith that keeps covenant with peoples all over the earth has to live in the tension between the historic struggle toward global unity and the natural differentiation of the planet. This is not easy for the churches of the North Atlantic, whose rehearsal of faith has bound Jesus' birth to the solstice of winter nighttime and the resurrection to the emergence of new plant growth in spring. A global covenant calls this reduction into question. It certainly unsettles a vast repertoire of songs and phrases that depend on these seasonal connections! In the words of one song, we northerners need to "sing a nativity summer can reach."[2]

Our second step is to look at the actual drama that is played out in the church year to see if this is indeed the dramatic scenario that lies at the heart of our longing for God's republic to flourish in our lives. In order to get at this question we have to examine our inherited liturgical year in a critical manner. Such an examination is on the radical side of the principle of radical gradualism that characterizes reform of worship.

The inherited liturgical year runs essentially from Advent to Pentecost. At the heart of this sequence is the drama of Jesus' life, which runs from Christmas to Easter. From the standpoint of a governance theory of worship, what do we see in this classic liturgical drama? The readings from Isaiah set up our political expectation within the framework of the renewal of God's promise to reconstitute the monarchy of

David in a dramatically new way. Our hope for ultimate justice is cast within the ancient visions of monarchical rule. This prophetic vision focuses on the expectation of the birth of a liberating king.

The Christmas celebration of the birth of this royal Messiah has to draw primarily on Matthew and Luke's infancy narrative. John's Gospel, drawing on both Greek philosophy and Jewish Wisdom traditions, sees this birth as the incarnation of the divine logos. Mark and St. Paul make no mention of the details of Jesus' birth, since their interests lie in his function in the drama of salvation. Both Matthew and Luke have to struggle to place Jesus' birth in Bethlehem rather than Nazareth so he can be descended from the House of David. What we have in Jesus' birth is the birth of a king—a messianic monarch. The coming of this Davidic Messiah can be established at birth, because inherited kingship (which is the model here) is a matter of biology rather than election. While Jesus' Davidic claims run through Joseph, his father is placed in an ambiguous paternal position so that Mary might be impregnated by a kind of divine consort—the Holy Spirit. The model of womanhood is thus attached to motherhood, the Holy Spirit is a mediator for the divine-human couple, and the governance of Christ is bound to genealogy and biology.

Thus, Christmas is not merely an accommodation to Roman Saturnalia and northern solstices but to the paradigm of inherited monarchy. As Handel's *Messiah* so powerfully presents it—with many musicians in his train—Christmas is a rehearsal of the birth of a new king, indeed the King of kings and Lord of lords.

The liturgical year then takes us through Jesus' ministry, half of which is cast within the folds of Lent—the product of European winters as well as monastic asceticism. Lent's self-sacrificing asceticism constitutes a long prologue to the crucifixion of Jesus, which is the exemplary sacrificial act. From the standpoint of Anselm's classic eleventh-century work *Cur Deus Homo*, the one whom we know in his birth as truly the crown prince must suffer and die to satisfy the honor of his father, the king. In Passion Week we rehearse a paradigm of the inheritance of monarchical authority. In each case, however, it is the reception of authority through complete and utter subordination to "the will of the father." That is, the son, though born a king, must prove himself worthy to reign. His self-sacrifice profoundly ratifies the hierarchy of patriarchal authority by which he will then rule. It is this paradigm that has characterized Christianity's relationship to governance throughout the era of Christendom.

The Easter resurrection is the successful outcome to this ratification of hierarchy's self-sacrifice. Through this death of the crown prince, and indeed his utter rejection of such royal pretenses, his true devotion to the system of governance, that is, to the father's will, is proved. The subsequent "ascension" to the father, after the symbolically rich forty-day presence with his people, completes his victorious negotiation of the drama of legitimate governance. He takes the throne—still evidently a crown prince at the father's right hand—and engages in the governmental task of judgment.

Only after the completion of this governance cycle is the Holy Spirit released, as the Western church came to put it, "from the Father and the Son" to create the assembly of believers that shall flow throughout the planet. However, in this traditional perspective the Holy Spirit's work at Pentecost does not reflect a new governance model; it is rather the fruits of Christ's reign in the ultimate scheme of things. The work of the Holy Spirit enables people to fit into the divine monarchy or, in Paul's conception, into the body whose head is Christ.

At that point Christians have traditionally finished the rehearsal of their drama of salvation. The season of Pentecost wanders on through the northern summer, with some subsequent celebration of the Trinity—itself traditionally a symbol of patriarchal and monarchical governance, despite the salute to the Holy Spirit. In this century, as a result of the upheavals of governance in Europe's twentieth-century fascist terror, the liturgical churches created the feast of Christ the King. While this November liturgy seeks to make relative all the totalitarian claims to ultimacy that have arisen in the collapse of Western Christendom, as a paradigm of governance it simply rehearses an order that has already collapsed as a pattern of legitimate governance. Shortly after this final salute to monarchy the cycle begins again with the messianic expectations of Advent.

In its bold outlines our present traditional liturgical year rehearses classic paradigms of divine kingship. Jesus' actual ministry and the outpouring of spirit that generated the church are clearly dependent on and subordinate to the saga of the self-sacrificing crown prince. The liturgical year invites us into a drama in which governors are known through birth rather than through election and covenantal agreement of the people. It then rehearses the hierarchy of paternal command by which monarchical authority is transferred. Even the ways that Jesus explicitly rejects in word and deed this monarchical framework has become part of the paradigm of self-denial and humility.

This, however, is not the world of political aspiration and faith by which most of us are trying to live. We are not longing for fresh messiahs and monarchs but for a more perfect Constitution, for a Congress that can debate in truth rather than deception, for a president who can discern and defend the core of wisdom in the conversation of the people, and for courts that uphold human rights rather than the clever games of lawyers. This is the actual governance faith that sustains us, and it also is rooted in the soil of the biblical heritage, even though for centuries it was seen as weeds between the pavement rather than the flowering of the garden's lushest trees.

How, then, might we reconstruct the liturgical year to reflect and rehearse this paradigm of governance, just as the worship we envisioned seeks to do on a weekly basis? Clearly Pentecost stands at the center of the creation of the Christian ecclesia—an assembly of people who are empowered to speak through the diversity of their languages to envision an ultimate republic of peaceful power. This means that the Holy Spirit is not simply a derivative of the Father-Son monarchical relationship but indeed is our central conception of the Divine itself. Thus, Pentecost, not Christmas or Easter, is the pivot point of the liturgical year.

Pentecost does, however, reach back to Easter, not as the conclusion of a monarchical drama begun earlier but as a cosmic regeneration based on analogy to the Passover and Exodus. The Easter Passover is the feast of liberation by which we enter into a promised land that is not merely geographical but cosmic. It begins to generate a special kind of public that is inaugurated by the teaching and ministry of Jesus, but which at Pentecost begins to unfold as a kind of political new creation. This public is grounded in gratitude for the gift of a new kind of public order of liberated conversation in which people can express and confirm their lives. It is grounded in the explosive emergence of a saving public rather than in the obedient self-sacrifice of the royal son to the will of the father.

Neither of these liturgical moments is bound to the seasons of the hemispheres, though each might sink its roots into its natural environment in different ways. More strikingly, they have much clearer roots in Jewish life. They are grafted on to Passover and Pentecost rather than Saturnalia and Augustan monarchy. This demands an ongoing conversation with Judaism, to be sure, since Christians and contemporary Jews differ about how to interpret this ancient heritage. Such an argument among equals, however, is better than the estrangement and Christian-inspired terrors of the past.

Such a re-centering of the liturgical year only begins the task, whose end I cannot envision. In the United States, for instance, it would require that we fill the traditional vacuum after Pentecost with appropriate festivals where the civil holidays of Memorial Day, Independence Day, Veterans Day, and Thanksgiving have sprung up in the doldrums of the churches' present practices. In other countries and regions the challenges will differ. How the political drama of Pentecost and its attendant dramas are interwoven with the seasonal dramas of the natural world have to be thought through anew. All I have tried to do here is set the course for a long journey.

CHAPTER EIGHT

Ethical Challenges of Worship Reform

THE REHEARSAL OF God's promised perfect public both forms our individual character and personalities as well as establishes commonly held images of proper authority and power. These rituals shape us as persons and can contribute to the basis for legitimate authority in public institutions. In saying we "pray for God's republic," we emphasize that this perfected public is a reality yet to come. We acknowledge that our present life is always a mere anticipation of the ultimate relationships of trust that save our fragile and finite life. In praying for God's republic we also commit ourselves into the roles, scripts, and actions appropriate to that public in which the God active in Jesus' ministry presides. We start living into that kind of public, where our true citizenship resides. These are the two central meanings to saying that worship is always an eschatological act—a rehearsal of our coming ultimate relation with God.

QUESTIONS SUCH WORSHIP RAISES

The shift in language and symbolism I am advancing here necessarily gives rise to some insistent questions. While much is familiar in the worship fantasy of the last chapter, much jars against our accustomed sensibilities. Such an experience raises many questions about the reform of worship along these lines. I will deal with only four of those questions here. The first question involves the integrity of monarchical worship traditions within cultures organized along monarchical lines. The second deals with the question of church governance implied by this kind of worship. The third takes up the question of the danger of idolatry in a world of republican civil religions. The fourth deals with the everyday practices required by a worship that is genuinely praying for God's republic.

Some critics of these proposals about worship might argue that they do not give due attention to the legitimate plurality of cultural traditions and the validity of the social structures they sustain. These proposals can be criticized simply as the expression of American political experience in light of its Puritan and Evangelical European heritage. As the product of largely North Atlantic inheritance they no more escape their European ethnic cocoon than the monarchical worship cultures they challenge. In fact, these proposals can be seen merely as expressions of the dominance of this racial-cultural group. They can be seen as actively undermining not only the monarchical worship paradigms in churches deriving from African, Asian, and Hispanic traditions but also the actual social structures legitimated by those worship patterns. In short, they do not sufficiently honor the ways in which various cultures symbolically anticipate a coming divine order of governance.

This criticism certainly identifies the history through which I have received these democratic, republican, and federal commitments. It is a flawed and fragile heritage. As with all human symbols, those of democracy and republican order have disguised exercises of domination and empire. No symbol can constrain our boundless capacities for evil. However, the value of these proposals needs to be assessed apart from the history of these symbols alone. Merely identifying their history and the functions they have played falls short of two important issues.

First, while it is important to honor the integrity of cultural patterns, we must remember that no ethnic or cultural tradition is monolithic. Just as the dominantly monarchical tradition of European Christendom carried within it the subordinate traditions of conciliarism, covenant, and democracy, so do other traditions. In particular, I am thinking of the village councils throughout Africa, which have always contested with monarchical developments, some of them introduced by European colonialists.[1] Thus, these proposals should be taken as invitations for people within dominantly patriarchal and monarchical traditions and cultures to recover and recast the forms in which people longed for a more public voice and participation in their own histories. How this might happen in our various ethnic and cultural traditions can only emerge through efforts at recovery and innovation in a variety of ethnic contexts.

Second, both majority and minority ethnic groups confront the challenge of living together in justice and peace, but how is this cultural and political plurality to be sustained in a common world? Principles of ethnic integrity and national sovereignty cannot themselves sustain such a quest for peace in plurality. These two principles alone have inevitably led to an effort to absorb the whole world into one ethnicity, race, or nationhood as the means to achieve peace. In our own century we have seen the terrible toll these ethnic-nationalist principles have taken on human life and on the natural world. The way to peace within a world of many cultures and varieties of human organization is through councils, covenants, federations, and the development of manifold publics of democratic participation. This does not erase the variety; indeed, it depends on it for the content of the wider republic of arguments and agreements. Moreover, the preservation of our unique cultural and ethnic traditions requires the establishment of such wider publics and covenants of mutual respect. Similarly, if our worship is to be a prayer for this wider peace it has to press us beyond not only our kinships but also our kingdoms to a vision of a republic where we all have a voice and a vote. The worship in which we entertain this vision needs to rehearse as well as motivate us to participate in this pluralistic republic of God's purposes.

In doing so we not only entertain a hope, we come under judgment. In God's republic the previously domineering are brought low and the voiceless are lifted up so they can enter a discourse of genuine persuasion rather than submit to the bullying so characteristic of our history. In God's public, however, we also are challenged to extend a voice to women as well as men, young as well as old, strong as well as weak. The call to publicity constantly challenges us to transcend appeals to the characteristics of our biology as the basis for our participation in God's republic.

The second critical question involves the kind of church order that is legitimated by praying for God's republic. Just as it seeks to move beyond the monarchies of our world, so it seems to move beyond ecclesiastical monarchies as well. This is true. The only question is what kind of federal-republican form would such a general church have? The fantasy worship experience we described only hinted at this assembly's involvement with the globe's assembly of Christians, not to mention other assemblies sharing this spirit. It seemed to exhibit a kind of congregational organization, but could have occurred in a wide range of denominations. While this worship vision clearly demands a high degree of publicity for the local assembly, it also requires some kind of wider association. How that would be structured within an overall federal-republican commitment can vary, just as Canada, the United States, Switzerland, India, and South Africa differ constitutionally and politically. This worship proposal only lifts up certain characteristics (or, if you will, "marks" or "notes") of the church's genuine rehearsal of God's ultimate aim. The emergence of an ecclesiastical order faithful to the prayer for God's coming republic and covenantal order awaits our ongoing historical efforts.[2]

Third, the use of contemporary republican and democratic symbolism is always in danger of being absorbed into the various civil religions that secular nation-states inevitably develop to ground their constitutions in more ultimate loyalties. Christianity as well as modern Judaism arose from the civil religion, so to speak, of ancient Israel. Contained within those civil religions, of course, was always the dynamic tension between the prophets and the people, especially their monarchs. The prophets continually had to recall to the people that their ultimate loyalty is not to their elders and kings but to the God who deals with them faithfully in covenant. For Christians, this prophetic tension is then amplified by the awareness of the historical gap between our present world and the world to come. To collapse the ultimate republic of God with our own republics is idolatry. It was a typical form of idolatry in the era of monarchy and Christendom, and it remains so in a world of republics. That is why it is so important that our worship always acknowledge the temporal as well as the behavioral gap between our covenantal commitments and our current behavior.

On the other hand, sometimes the civil liturgies of our nations reflect the publics known in our Christian worship. Indeed, this mirroring properly manifests an intended impact of our worship activity. However, inasmuch as it is *national* ritual, it inherently falls short of God's wider republic. Our prayer for this ultimate republic must then always take care, even as it speaks much of the language of our common political aspirations, to preserve clear distinctions between our worship as citizens of God's republic and our participation in our civil cults. Indeed, at many points participation in these civic rituals and practices may contradict what we profess in the Christian assembly. At some point we always face the decision to refrain from those civic practices, whether in sports, politics, the military, or education, even or especially when they mimic the rituals of our ultimate commitments.

The Underlying Question of Ritual Practices

Finally, I want to address what is perhaps the most important point of all. Indeed, it is a point underlying all the others. We must take care to see that our ritual practices are actually embedded in political and social practices that are congruent with our prayers. If members of the assembly are not also nurturing publicity for people who are otherwise voiceless and voteless, then they cannot with integrity express a genuine hope for God's republic in their worship. This requirement for congruence between worship and practice has always been the case, ever since Amos denounced the empty worship of ancient Israel and called for righteousness rather than empty and solemn rituals. It is no less the case for the worship forms advanced here. Assemblies that pray for God's republic have to work together to expand publicity, democratic participation, and covenantal trust in people's actual lives together in this creation. This little book cannot spell out this agenda on these pages. Such an agenda involves the traditional work of preserving the connections of prisoners with their families and communities, of keeping in public awareness people who are ill and housebound, and of struggling to bring the truth of our broken history to the public light. It urges advocacy for an otherwise silent natural world in the publics of our legislatures and courts. It embraces all those acts of teaching, housing, and healing that enable people to participate effectively in the publics around them. These are some of the practices of a people praying for God's republic. Without them even our most gripping ceremonies fall to the ground like gaudy but spent balloons.

These are some of the questions and concerns evoked by the proposal to regenerate our worship as a rehearsal of God's republic. There are doubtless many others that require an expanded public conversation. At this point others must take up the arguments and conversations out of which can emerge the kind of practices through which Christians, along with others, might find a voice for professing their faith and hope in a world struggling for a more adequate justice and peace.

A Conversation with President Jesus

THE WORSHIP FANTASY IN chapter 7 lifted up a complete worship experience as a way of getting the feel for a life of prayer lived in anticipation of God's republic. A different and more limited entry into this sensibility might be gained through the following encounter with Jesus as president. It can be performed in worship in preparation for Holy Communion as a monologue or as a "reader's theater" piece.

Two rocking chairs are placed near the communion table, facing each other or slightly at an angle, depending on where the people are seated. One chair is empty. The other is taken by the person speaking. After a silence the person in the rocker begins:

"Where have you been? You've been so hard to get a hold of, I'm not even sure I recognized you. One minute you're here, another you're gone. Are you really the one we elected? I know it sounds strange, but I'm not sure you're really our president at all. You'd think people would know their president, wouldn't you?

"I'm sorry. I didn't mean to be rude. You just don't seem to understand how hard it's been for us. We had such hopes for you. You won the election against all odds. The polls were all wrong, as usual. They never imagined that someone from your hometown could do it . . . I'm sorry about that reference . . . But we were so fired up . . .

"But then . . . word of your torture and assassination . . . we were shattered . . . dazed . . .

"We couldn't believe it when you showed up at the inaugural ball, and then at the meeting upstairs—or was it a party? We were so ecstatic about your presence that all the differences of the campaign were bridged. We could really talk with each other again. We understood each other for the first time. You were there. You were our president. Your power was everywhere! We could really feel your presence and authority!

"But then you just disappeared. A couple of people said they had seen you, even had lunch with you at the diner. But that was it. [*Speaker stands.*]

"We had real hopes then. A whole new miraculous era was opening up. And you promised us so much—a New Covenant, you said. A new federalism. More power to the people where they really live. More power to local groups who can really talk with one another and work things out. They wouldn't have to depend on distant bureaucrats and politicians who wouldn't listen to them.

"But without your leadership we just pulled all those plans back into the black hole of our petty interests. We never could get the big picture again without your help. Then the disappointments started.

"Let me put it this way. In a way, you overcame assassination, but you couldn't overcome our self-interests, our weaknesses, our vicious fears, our pettiness, our arrogance. The old factions regrouped; life seemed to return to its usual derelictions.

"We were hoping that you could make us do better. Take charge, like a real president! . . . Yeah, I know, the congress. I don't see why you trust them more than us. They don't get the picture, the "insider vision" you let us have. For that matter, I don't know why you trust us either. Instead of giving clear commands to clean up this mess, you let us wander off on our own, telling us to take responsibility—act as if *we* were the ones who had been elected. Well, we can't do it! You know that! We've proved it to you over and over. We're simply irresponsible!

"Where *have* you been? All those horrible things that happened—incredible exploitation in mines and factories, enslavement, segregation, apartheid, genocide, plagues and pogroms, and wars beyond counting (many in your name)—why couldn't you stop us? Where were you? Isn't that what we elected you for?

"And you just sit there rocking, speaking in whispers or not at all . . . Well, at least *we're* here . . . well, *some* of us. A couple of people had relatives visiting. They weren't members of our party, so they said they couldn't bring them. I know Bruce had to get his car fixed. There's an important meeting in town to deal with some sewer problems . . . Okay, I'm sorry we don't have a better turnout . . . People are busy. They're keeping things going while you just sit in that rocker.

"Okay, we'll work on the mailing list. Probably had some computer glitches. We'll have a better turnout next time. We'll get *everyone* here. But you have to let us know when you're coming. You can't just show up unexpected like this!

"You say we *are* all here? How? Well, yes, we do have the evidence— right on us . . . the cloth from India. Cheap, they're made by children in the villages. Yes, the shirt, China, cheap labor there, too; prisoners they say. Yes, the cars from Detroit and Japan, I hear there's one from Germany. The license plates are made by prisoners too.

"You call them . . . your constituents? You're *their* president too? All? But they didn't vote for you. I mean, it would be unconstitutional. They weren't properly registered! Well, you never did have much respect for our constitution. Too limited, you always said. Didn't include everybody. You just have no sense of proper jurisdiction! You act like boundaries don't matter!

"And yes, what *about* you? Why are we always dwelling on *our* shortcomings? Here we elected you. You said you would be our servant. Servanthood was in for you. You promised to stick with us—something that's never happened in the history of any presidency. People still can't figure it out. Now, well, you invited us here and I don't even see a sign of the refreshments! [*Move toward rocker.*]

"People say they've seen you. You were in line down at the soup kitchen just last week, exchanging your ham sandwich for peanut butter. They spotted you easily, a dead giveaway. And downtown at the bank, you were picketing, shouting for debt forgiveness for Third World countries—that Jubilee idea of yours. And you were at that fund-raiser in Grande Pointe last week. It's amazing how much you can charm out of those wealthy widows.

"But times are too desperate for this little stuff. It's time to knock off this grassroots business and get moving again! We know you're around, we'd just like you to take office like a real president—like a commander in chief.

"All we seem to have are all these vice presidents [*Gesture toward congregation.*], and they hardly ever have the kind of spirit you had. They just can't replace you. And with so many of them, how could we ever tell who would succeed you if . . . you . . . died? Well. What I mean is— I don't know what I mean—it's just a big mystery. We'll have to talk more about that. [*Tip rocker and walk away.*]

"All right, I've just been complaining. You've been listening patiently. I think that's the secret to the hold you have over us. Well, what *do* you expect of us? Not a little contribution? . . . later? Maybe after the coffee? You want more? Would ten percent be enough? You know, the Bible says . . . no? More? That's extortion, probably illegal. You want . . . our life? That's virtual slavery! Don't you know slavery is out? Don't you have any sense of limits? What are you, some kind of totalitarian dictator? We've got our rights! We are free citizens! I thought that was the basis of the whole arrangement!

"Anyway, what do *we* get out of it?

"Life? Life? That's it? You're promising us life? Free life? No, strings attached . . . There are strings attached.

"It has to be *here?* Here with the others? But I don't even know some of these people. They're strangers. About all we have in common is *you*, or the faint reports of your wanderings. Talk about a strange republic, this is surely it. And it's so fragile and fleeting. It's like puppy love and morning dew. It's like the mountain fog—impenetrable but insubstantial. Anyway, how can we ever get together? We're so completely different from each other!

"What? Come to the table, you say. Sit down at the round table. Meet and eat. Eat with strangers? But my mother always said . . . Frankly, we would rather pick up a video, crank up the VCR, hit the couch, and daze out. Now that's living, isn't it? Isn't that living? Aren't you there too? Nice intimate surroundings? . . . No?

"Is this where you want to meet us? Here in this assembly? Here is where you preside? These are your friends? You want to turn strangers into friends? But that's going to take time. It's difficult to be friends among strangers. You're asking a lot. This is hard—this searching and finding and losing and searching and hoping. People can get killed doing that. You'll have to be patient.

"I know you have to go. I have to go too. I just want one definite promise from you. You have my vote. I'll get some friends to vote for you too, but I beg you, be with us until it is finished. Be whatever kind of president you have to be, but preside with us. Please. I'll stay for the meal if you will. And they will . . . You can still be the host. Let's eat together again and you can talk with us about how your presidency is going to work out after all."

Guiding the Discussion

N<small>O CHANGES IN WORSHIP CAN</small> or should occur without a consensus rooted in reflection, discussion, debate, and a struggle for common solutions. This book is short, but it raises many difficult and emotion-laden questions. Behind its claims and questions lie centuries of disputation and development. As an aid to congregations and groups struggling with these issues I offer here some leading questions, arranged by chapter, for initiating discussions.

CHAPTER 1: BEYOND THE WORSHIP OF "KINGAFAP"

1. What position do you take or what gestures do you use when you are praying? Why?
2. What relationship to God and to other people do these positions or gestures imply?
3. Where is the Bible placed in your church during worship? What does this say about the location of authority in your congregation or church?
4. Do you have a procession when you worship? What order do people come in? What does this say about the authority and power relations in the church?
5. Reflect on the architecture and arrangement of furniture in your church. What does this arrangement imply for relationships of power and authority?
6. Has your congregation tried to change songs, prayers, or other parts of the worship to include references to both women and men? What questions and concerns arose in that effort?

7. Have you tried to change language relating to political imagery in worship? What happened, both for you and for others in your congregation?

8. What other changes have you tried to make in symbolism, ritual, or architecture for the sake of ethical values such as inclusiveness, equality, or accessibility? What issues did these changes pose for people?

CHAPTER 2: THE NEED FOR INTEGRITY IN WORSHIP

1. Are there parts of your worship you would like to see changed? Why?

2. Are there parts of your worship you think should never be changed under any circumstance? Why?

3. How do you see Christian worship relating to Jewish traditions and to Judaism? What is being said ethically in this way of relating the two worship traditions?

4. Where in your worship do you anticipate and hope for God's promised new order? What form does this expression take?

CHAPTER 3: WORSHIP AS POLITICAL REHEARSAL

1. What do you think is the purpose of worship? How are the three purposes of motivation, education, and presentation involved in your typical worship? Which is dominant? Why?

2. What do you think of the idea that worship is a kind of "rehearsal" of our relationship with God, others, and all of creation? What are the dramatic parts of your worship? What kinds of relationships are they "rehearsing"?

3. Do you have an American or a state flag in your sanctuary? Why or why not? How close or distant is your worship to the "civil religion" around you?

4. Read I Samuel 8 and reflect on the choice the leaders of Israel made then. What does their dilemma mean for us today?

5. Make a list of the titles given to Jesus in the New Testament and identify their political meaning. What other titles might we have added if we were writing the Gospels today?

Chapter 4: Sunday Monarchists and Monday Citizens

1. Leaf through your congregation's hymnal and see how it uses the language of feudalism, monarchy, and fatherhood. What emotions does this language arouse in you? What parts of your life does it connect with? What parts does it not connect with? Do you agree with this chapter's claim that people only connect this monarchical language to psychological or domestic aspects of their lives?

2. Imagine celebrating Christmas or Easter without using any references to kings, princes, or lords. How would these celebrations be different?

3. What differences do you sense when you refer to God as Mother rather than as Father?

4. How does your worship use symbols from the natural world? What models of relationship do they rehearse?

Chapter 5: Choosing the Political Imagery of Our Worship

1. What are the major ethical differences between using parenthood and family as the model for governance and using councils and democracy?

2. Make a list of all the words and ideas that connect with the idea of "public" today—phrases like "going public" or "publicity." Where do they connect with your daily life? Reflect on the tension between private and public aspects of your life. What aspects of publicity frighten you? What aspects encourage or confirm you?

3. What does the idea of a republic mean in your own history and in that of your country? Why are people trying to create or improve republics and democracies in the world today?

4. Reflect on the differences between the language of "rule," "presidency," and "governance." What important differences exist among them? How do these differences appear in worship?

5. Reflect on the strengths and limits of the symbolism of fatherhood and divine sonship as distinguished from that of election when referring to God and Christ.

6. What is the difference between a bond of covenant and one of kinship? How might they be related? Where do you see covenant-like forms of association in public life? What is the connection between covenant and federal constitutionalism? Why are covenantal bonds important for republics?

7. Are there patterns of covenant rehearsal in your present worship? How are they ritualized? How do they function in your worship life?

8. For Christians, the spirit of Christ is to govern the assembly at worship. How is this manifested in your own patterns of Christian worship? What are other ways that God's governance is made known in worship?

9. Why is musical form so central to how people worship? What ethical values do different types of music and instruments convey?

CHAPTER 6: SOME GUIDING PRINCIPLES FOR REGENERATING WORSHIP

1. What pattern of participation shapes your worship? What characterizes the relationships among the participants? What principle of representation determines who participates in leadership roles? Who is excluded from participation? How?

2. What is the ideal size for a worshiping congregation? What principles govern your decision about size?

3. What covenants or covenant-like agreements "constitute" your congregation or your church? How are they rehearsed? How does this rehearsal reflect a theory of power and authority?

4. Where, in your present worship, do you think your worship practices mirror too closely the world around you? Where are they too distant and irrelevant?

5. Reflect carefully on the book's purpose of providing a "language and grammar" for worship rather than a set of symbols that will provide *the* right way of speaking theologically. What does this difference mean for the question of hope and of idolatry?

6. How do you see the connection between the way you rear children and the way you think government should work? How do your

worship practices reflect the connection between the two spheres of life?

7. Which senses are most important for you in worship? How does this shape the way you approach the actual worship practices of your congregation? What role do the various senses play in shaping the way we relate to each other and to institutions?

8. How do the two concerns of avoiding idolatry (the "Protestant" impulse) and manifesting the incarnation of God (the "Catholic" impulse) shape your worship? Which is most important? Why?

CHAPTER 7: PRAYING FOR GOD'S REPUBLIC: A WORSHIP FANTASY

1. How would you rewrite Jesus' prayer to reflect democratic and constitutional models of governance?

2. Reflect further on the difference between lordship and presidency. What ethical values underlie the choice between the two terms in worship?

3. What is the most striking part of the worship fantasy for you? What ethical values does it project?

4. What does it mean for us to say baptism is a ritual of citizenship?

5. What aspects of the fantasy could most easily be introduced into your worship? Which are most difficult?

6. Explore the implications of the circular architecture of the worship space for how speech and music are carried on. What other aspects of worship does circularity affect?

7. How does your worship reflect the relation of Christianity to Judaism? How might it express this relationship better?

8. Where, on ethical or theological grounds, should the center of the church year lie? How does your church interrelate the natural seasons with its church year? What does this connection say for our ethical stance toward the natural world?

9. How should Christians celebrate Pentecost?

CHAPTER 8: ETHICAL CHALLENGES OF WORSHIP REFORM

1. What differences do you see in the way symbols of patriarchy and monarchy function in traditionally white or black churches, in Hispanic, or in Asian churches? How might the arguments set forth in this book work out in the various contexts? What issues do these proposals present in these different cultural contexts?

2. What connections do you see between the way your church or congregation worships and the structures of the organization it is governed by?

3. Have you ever experienced occasions when your religious commitments held you back from participating in rituals connected with government, military life, sports, education, or other important institutions? What did you do about it?

4. What is your congregation or church doing to promote people's participation in their governing publics? How is this reflected in the way you worship?

Notes

Preface

1. *God's Federal Republic: Reconstructing Our Governing Symbol* (New York: Paulist Press, 1988).

1. Beyond the Worship of "Kingafap"

1. Brian Wren, *What Language Shall I Borrow? God-Talk in Worship: A Male Response to Feminist Theology* (New York: Crossroad, 1989), 119–30, 227–35.

2. *The New Century Hymnal* (Cleveland: The Pilgrim Press, 1995), no. 304. Original words by Edward Perronet.

3. *The New Century Hymnal*, no. 312. Adapted by Lavon Bayler.

4. Wren, *What Language Shall I Borrow?* 134 ff.

2. The Need for Integrity in Worship

1. For a general introduction see James F. White, *Introduction to Christian Worship* (Nashville: Abingdon Press, 1980). For the classic Anglican study of the Eucharist see Dom Gregory Dix, *The Shape of the Liturgy*, 2d ed. (London: Dacre Press, Adam & Charles Black, [1945] 1975).

2. For important sources of contemporary liturgical reconstruction see V. Turner, *The Ritual Process: Structure and Anti-structure* (Chicago: Aldine Publishing Company, 1969), and Mary Douglas, *Natural Symbols: Explorations in Cosmology* (New York: Pantheon Books, [1973] 1982).

3. Don E. Saliers, *Worship as Theology: Foretaste of Divine Glory* (Nashville: Abingdon Press, 1994). See also his *Worship Come to Its Senses* (Nashville: Abingdon Press, 1996).

4. "Stars and Planets Flung in Orbit," by Herman G. Stuempfle, in *The New Century Hymnal*, no. 567.

5. See Saliers, *Worship as Theology* , and his citation of Alexander Schmemann, *Introduction to Liturgical Theology* (New York: St. Vladimir's Seminary Press, 1966), 13.

6. Vigen Guroian, "Seeing Worship as Ethics," in *Incarnate Love* (Notre Dame, Ind.: University of Notre Dame Press, 1987), 51–78.

7. Vigen Guroian, *Ethics after Christendom: Toward an Ecclesial Christian Ethic* (Grand Rapids, Mich.: Eerdmans, 1994), esp. 83–101.

8. Stanley Hauerwas, *A Community of Character: Toward a Constructive Christian Social Ethic* (Notre Dame, Ind.: University of Notre Dame, 1981), and John Westerhoff, *Living the Faith Community: The Church That Makes a Difference* (Minneapolis: Winston Press, 1985).

9. See my earlier reflections in William J. Everett, "Liturgy and American Society: An Invocation to Ethical Analysis," *Anglican Theological Review* 56 (January 1974): 16–34.

10. Peter Berger, *The Sacred Canopy: Elements of a Sociological Theory of Religion* (Garden City, N.Y.: Doubleday-Anchor, 1969), 127–53.

11. See Adrian Cunningham, Terry Eagleton, Brian Wicker, et al., *The Slant Manifesto: Catholics and the Left* (Springfield, Ill.: Templegate Publishers, 1966), 31–37, 148–82, and Brian Wicker, *First the Political Kingdom: A Personal Appraisal of the Catholic Left in Britain* (Notre Dame, Ind.: University of Notre Dame Press, 1967), 81–90.

12. Richard Sennett, *The Fall of Public Man: On the Social Psychology of Capitalism* (New York: Random House-Vintage, 1978), 3–6. For a rich comparison of Anglo and Hispanic approaches to "publicity" see Glen Claudill Dealy, *The Public Man: An Interpretation of Latin American and Other Catholic Countries* (Amherst: University of Massachusetts Press, 1977).

13. The increasingly influential work of Hannah Arendt lies behind much of my thinking about publicity. See especially her *The Human Condition* (Garden City, N.Y.: Doubleday, 1959) and *On Revolution* (New York: Viking Press, 1965).

14. For a rich background on this development see Daniel J. Elazar, *Covenant and Polity in Biblical Israel*, vol. 1 of *The Covenant Tradition in Politics* (New Brunswick, N.J.: Transaction Publishers, 1995).

15. See, for instance, the classic Vatican statement on the ordination of women in "Declaration on Certain Questions Concerning Sexual Ethics ("Persona Humana")," *Sacred Congregation for the Doctrine of the Faith*, Dec. 29, 1975.

16. Timothy Sedgwick, *Sacramental Ethics* (Philadelphia: Fortress Press, 1987), and Harmon L. Smith, *Where Two or Three Are Gathered: Liturgy and the Moral Life* (Cleveland: The Pilgrim Press, 1995).

17. For an extended discussion of this problem and its practical ramifications see Ruth C. Duck, *Gender and the Name of God: The Trinitarian Baptismal Formula* (New York: The Pilgrim Press, 1991).

3. WORSHIP AS POLITICAL REHEARSAL

1. Saliers, *Worship as Theology*, passim.

2. Sallie McFague has been especially helpful in exploring this feature of theology. See her *Metaphorical Theology: Models of God in Religious Language* (Philadelphia: Fortress

Press, 1982) and *The Body of God: An Ecological Theology* (Minneapolis: Augsburg/Fortress Press, 1993). My proposals here, however, take a different tack in the actual choice of metaphors for organizing theology and worship.

3. Paul Tillich, "The Religious Symbol," in *Myth and Symbol*, ed. Frederick W. Dillistone (London: SPCK, 1966), 15–34.

4. SUNDAY MONARCHISTS AND MONDAY CITIZENS

1. I pursued some of these questions, with a bit of attention to worship issues, in *Religion, Federalism, and the Struggle for Public Life: Cases from Germany, India, and America* (New York: Oxford University Press, 1997).

2. See William Holladay, *The Psalms through Three Thousand Years: Prayerbook of a Cloud of Witnesses* (Minneapolis: Augsburg/Fortress Press, 1993).

3. Eusebius, "Oration on the Tricennalia of Constantine," quoted in Henry Myers, *Medieval Kingship* (Chicago: Nelson-Hall, 1982), 25.

4. *The United Methodist Hymnal*, no. 399 (Nashville: Abingdon Press, 1989).

5. Ann Douglas, *The Feminization of American Culture* (New York: Knopf, 1977); A. Gregory Schneider, *The Way of the Cross Leads Home: The Domestication of American Methodism* (Bloomington: Indiana University Press, 1993); and Janet Forsythe Fishburn, *The Fatherhood of God and the Victorian Family: The Social Gospel in America* (Philadelphia: Fortress Press, 1981).

6. This utopian antipolitical stance is now being corrected by feminist political thinkers such as Jean Bethke Elshtain. See, for instance, her *Private Man, Public Woman: Women in Social and Political Thought* (Princeton, N.J.: Princeton University Press, 1981).

7. This is a prominent theme in Sallie McFague's *The Body of God*.

5. CHOOSING THE POLITICAL IMAGERY OF OUR WORSHIP

1. Murray's understanding of public life is also central to my framework. See his *We Hold These Truths: Catholic Reflections on the American Proposition* (Garden City, N.Y.: Doubleday-Image, 1964) and, for a fine discussion, see Leon Hooper, *The Ethics of Discourse: The Social Philosophy of John Courtney Murray* (Washington, D.C.: Georgetown University Press, 1986).

2. Kinship persists in Judaism as a principle for relating successive generations to the original covenant representatives of Israel, but this does not contest the voluntary character of the covenant itself. Whether this voluntarism should also determine who participates in this covenant is an ongoing debate within Judaism. See the essays in Daniel J. Elazar, ed., *Kinship and Consent* (Ramat Gan, Israel: Turtledove, 1981).

3. I cannot here go into the many ways the Trinity of "persons" has been used to articulate both patriarchal rule and succession as well as notions of tripartite governance and many other governance models! There are significant issues in choosing

among these interpretations. My only point is to avoid the reduction of the Trinity to a matter of privacy and intimacy. For an extended discussion of this issue see Elizabeth Johnson, *She Who Is: The Mystery of God in Feminist Theological Discourse* (New York: Crossroad, 1992).

4. This is a key idea in Harmon Smith's *Where Two or Three Are Gathered*. See also William J. Everett and Thomas E. Frank, "Constitutional Order in United Methodism and American Culture," in *Connectionalism: Ecclesiology, Mission, and Identity*, ed. Russell E. Richey, Dennis M. Campbell, and William B. Lawrence, United Methodism in American Culture series, vol. I (Nashville: Abingdon Press, 1997), 41–73.

6. SOME GUIDING PRINCIPLES FOR REGENERATING WORSHIP

1. Joseph Allen, *Love and Conflict: Toward a Covenantal Ethic* (Lanham, Md.: University Press of America, 1995).

2. See Janet Fishburn, *The Fatherhood of God and the Victorian Family*, and Peter Paris, *The Social Teaching of the Black Churches* (Nashville: Abingdon Press, 1985), 10.

3. This return of the body in worship needs to avoid, however, the fixation on "perfect" bodies that pervades not only our own culture but the biblical heritage as well. For sensitive reflections on a deeper awareness of the bodiliness of worship see the essays in Nancy L. Eisland and Don E. Saliers, eds., *Human Disability and the Service of God: Reassessing Religious Practice* (Nashville: Abingdon Press, 1998).

4. For a deeper look at the tension and necessary connection between the "Protestant Principle" and Catholic sacramental emphases see Paul Tillich, "Nature and Sacrament" and "The Protestant Message and the Man of Today," in *The Protestant Era*, trans. James L. Adams (Chicago: University of Chicago Press, 1948), 94–112, 192–205, and James Luther Adams's essay "Tillich's Concept of the Protestant Era" in the same volume (esp. 288–305).

7. PRAYING FOR GOD'S REPUBLIC: A WORSHIP FANTASY

1. For extended reflections on worship in the round see Letty Russell, *The Church in the Round* (Louisville: Westminster/John Knox, 1993).

2. From "Carol Our Christmas," by Shirley E. Murray, in *The New Century Hymnal*, no. 141.

8. ETHICAL CHALLENGES OF WORSHIP REFORM

1. See the critical inquiries of Basil Davidson, *The Black Man's Burden: Africa and the Curse of the Nation-State* (New York: Times Books, 1992), and Mahmood Mamdani, *Citizen and Subject: Contemporary Africa and the Legacy of Late Colonialism* (Princeton, N.J.: Princeton University Press, 1996).

2. For an imaginative start see the earlier contributions to a global ecclesiology by the present general secretary of the World Council of Churches, Konrad Raiser, *Ecumenism in Transition: A Paradigm Shift in the Ecumenical Movement?*, trans. Tony Coates (Geneva: WCC Publications, 1991).

Related Books from United Church Press and The Pilgrim Press

THE NEW CENTURY PSALTER

Burton H. Throckmorton Jr. and Arthur G. Clyde, eds.

The New Century Psalter completes the groundbreaking work begun by *The New Century Hymnal,* providing worshiping communities and individuals with all 150 psalms in inclusive language. The verses are arranged in balanced couplets for easy reading, and each psalm is presented in pointed form for singing in worship. Includes suggestions for using psalms in daily devotions, orders for both community and individual morning and evening prayer, and directions for singing the psalms and antiphons. 1361-6 / 256 pages
Cloth / $14.95

PREACHING JUSTICE
Ethnic and Cultural Perspectives

Christine Marie Smith, ed.

This innovative book takes pastors and other readers inside the circle of eight ethnic and cultural communities—persons with disabilities, Native Americans, African Americans, Filipino Americans, Hispanics, Korean Americans, Jews, and lesbians and gays—in order to experience a portion of their lives and thus preach to them from a position of understanding and compassion. The act of doing theology is made concrete and personal as each writer moves from identifying the elements of oppression to lifting up symbols of justice and liberation. 1291-1 / 176 pages
Paper / $14.95

AND EVERYONE SHALL PRAISE
Resources for Multicultural Worship

R. Mark Liebenow

And Everyone Shall Praise is a bountiful resource designed for worship leaders who want to engage their congregation in multicultural and multiracial worship. Liturgies, responsive readings, prayers, stories, and poems for use in worship are presented, and a helpful calendar of major church observances—including a number of social justice events—is provided. The book also contains guidelines and suggestions to encourage worship leaders to write their own liturgical materials.

1318-7 / 256 pages
Paper / $19.95

THE COLOR OF FAITH
Building Community in a Multiracial Society

Fumitaka Matsuoka

Race relations is one of this nation's major concerns. How can congregations and their leaders forge a new vision of relatedness and community building across racial divides? Matsuoka's timely book provides a theological perspective on racial and ethnic plurality, with its sharpest focus on the alienation that surrounds shifting race lines and the connection between race and justice.

1281-4 / 144 pages
Paper / $15.95

FUTURING YOUR CHURCH
Finding Your Vision and Making It Work

George B. Thompson Jr.

"This hands-on, step-by-step approach should give every church leader new confidence in the practical possibilities of renewal in their ministry." —Carl S. Dudley

Thompson leads church leaders through an exploration of their congregation's heritage, its current context, and its theological bearings. From the insights gleaned, members can discern their church's vision—what God is currently calling the church to do in this time and place. Thompson then provides a simple organization model for applying the vision and making it work.

1331-4 / 128 pages
Paper / $14.95

DOING THE TWIST TO AMAZING GRACE

Alice Ogden Bellis

Often humorous, always engaging, Bellis shares her personal experiences and keen biblical insights to stimulate worshipers, as well as those reentering the church, to gather up their faith experiences and faith understanding, leading them to deeper, more mature expressions of faith. Study questions are included.

1273-3 / 128 pages
Paper / $9.95

CONGREGATION
The Journey Back to Church

Gary Dorsey

"A masterpiece of journalism." —M. Scott Peck

Dorsey lets us peer into the hearts of ordinary people leading extraordinary spiritual lives. Yet only in a moment of personal crisis does he begin his own search for a spiritual home within the church community in this compassionate, funny, and deeply moving account of mainstream Protestant life today.

1296-2 / 400 pages
Paper / $18.95

To order these or any other book from United Church Press or
The Pilgrim Press please call or write to:

The Pilgrim Press/United Church Press
700 Prospect Avenue East
Cleveland OH 44115-1100

Phone orders: 1-800-537-3394
Fax orders: 216-736-3713

Please include shipping charges of $3.50 for the first book and
$0.50 for each additional book.

Or order from our Web sites at www.ucpress.com and
www.pilgrimpress.com.

Prices subject to change without notice.